MODERN WORLD LEADERS

Viktor Yushchenko

MODERN WORLD LEADERS

Tony Blair
George W. Bush
Hugo Chávez
Jacques Chirac
Hamid Karzai
Hosni Mubarak
Pervez Musharraf
Pope Benedict XVI
Pope John Paul II
Vladimir Putin
The Saudi Royal Family
Ariel Sharon
Viktor Yushchenko

MODERN WORLD LEADERS

Viktor Yushchenko

Dennis Abrams

BRIDGEWATER, N.J. 08807

CHELSEA HOUSE
PUBLISHERS
An imprint of Infobase Publishing

Viktor Yushchenko

Chelsea House
An imprint of Infobase Publishing
132 West 31st Street
New York, NY 10001

ISBN-10: 0-7910-9266-6
ISBN-13: 978-0-7910-9266-8

Library of Congress Cataloging-in-Publication Data

Abrams, Dennis, 1960-
  Viktor Yushchenko / Dennis Abrams.
    p. cm. — (Modern world leaders)
  Includes bibliographical references and index.
  ISBN 0-7910-9266-6 (hardcover)
  1. IUshchenko, Viktor, 1954—Juvenile literature. 2. Presidents—Ukraine—Biography—Juvenile literature. 3. Ukraine—Politics and government—1991—Juvenile literature. 4. Ukraine—History—Juvenile literature. I. Title. II. Series.
  DK508.851.I89A27 2007
  947.708/6092 B22   2006032893

Text design by Erik Lindstrom
Cover design by Takeshi Takehashi

Printed in the United States of America

Bang EJB 10 9 8 7 6 5 4 3 2 1

This book is printed on acid-free paper.

TABLE OF CONTENTS

ARTHUR M. SCHLESINGER, JR.

On Leadership

Leadership, it may be said, is really what makes the world go round. Love no doubt smoothes the passage; but love is a private transaction between consenting adults. Leadership is a public transaction with history. The idea of leadership affirms the capacity of individuals to move, inspire, and mobilize masses of people so that they act together in pursuit of an end. Sometimes leadership serves good purposes, sometimes bad; but whether the end is benign or evil, great leaders are those men and women who leave their personal stamp on history.

Now, the very concept of leadership implies the proposition that individuals can make a difference. This proposition has never been universally accepted. From classical times to the present day, eminent thinkers have regarded individuals as no more than the agents and pawns of larger forces, whether the gods and goddesses of the ancient world or, in the modern era, race, class, nation, the dialectic, the will of the people, the spirit of the times, history itself. Against such forces, the individual dwindles into insignificance.

So contends the thesis of historical determinism. Tolstoy's great novel *War and Peace* offers a famous statement of the case. Why, Tolstoy asked, did millions of men in the Napoleonic Wars, denying their human feelings and their common sense, move back and forth across Europe slaughtering their fellows? "The war," Tolstoy answered, "was bound to happen simply because it was bound to happen." All prior history determined it. As for leaders, they, Tolstoy said, "are but the labels that serve to give a name to an end and, like labels, they have the least possible connection with the event." The greater the leader, "the more conspicuous the inevitability and the predestination of every act he commits." The leader, said Tolstoy, is "the slave of history."

Determinism takes many forms. Marxism is the determinism of class. Nazism the determinism of race. But the idea of men and women as the slaves of history runs athwart the deepest human instincts. Rigid determinism abolishes the idea of human freedom—the assumption of free choice that underlies every move we make, every word we speak, every thought we think. It abolishes the idea of human responsibility, since it is manifestly unfair to reward or punish people for actions that are by definition beyond their control. No one can live consistently by any deterministic creed. The Marxist states prove this themselves by their extreme susceptibility to the cult of leadership.

More than that, history refutes the idea that individuals make no difference. In December 1931, a British politician crossing Fifth Avenue in New York City between 76th and 77th streets around 10:30 P.M. looked in the wrong direction and was knocked down by an automobile—a moment, he later recalled, of a man aghast, a world aglare: "I do not understand why I was not broken like an eggshell or squashed like a gooseberry." Fourteen months later an American politician, sitting in an open car in Miami, Florida, was fired on by an assassin; the man beside him was hit. Those who believe that individuals make no difference to history might well ponder whether the next two decades would have been the same had Mario Constasino's car killed Winston Churchill in 1931 and Giuseppe Zangara's bullet killed Franklin Roosevelt in 1933. Suppose, in addition, that Lenin had died of typhus in Siberia in 1895 and that Hitler had been killed on the western front in 1916. What would the twentieth century have looked like now?

For better or for worse, individuals do make a difference. "The notion that a people can run itself and its affairs anonymously," wrote the philosopher William James, "is now well known to be the silliest of absurdities. Mankind does nothing save through initiatives on the part of inventors, great or small, and imitation by the rest of us—these are the sole factors in human progress. Individuals of genius show the way, and set the patterns, which common people then adopt and follow."

Leadership, James suggests, means leadership in thought as well as in action. In the long run, leaders in thought may well make the greater difference to the world. "The ideas of economists and political philosophers, both when they are right and when they are wrong," wrote John Maynard Keynes, "are more powerful than is commonly understood. Indeed the world is ruled by little else. Practical men, who believe themselves to be quite exempt from any intellectual influences, are usually the slaves of some defunct economist. . . . The power of vested interests is vastly exaggerated compared with the gradual encroachment of ideas."

But, as Woodrow Wilson once said, "Those only are leaders of men, in the general eye, who lead in action. . . . It is at their hands that new thought gets its translation into the crude language of deeds." Leaders in thought often invent in solitude and obscurity, leaving to later generations the tasks of imitation. Leaders in action—the leaders portrayed in this series—have to be effective in their own time.

And they cannot be effective by themselves. They must act in response to the rhythms of their age. Their genius must be adapted, in a phrase from William James, "to the receptivities of the moment." Leaders are useless without followers. "There goes the mob," said the French politician, hearing a clamor in the streets. "I am their leader. I must follow them." Great leaders turn the inchoate emotions of the mob to purposes of their own. They seize on the opportunities of their time, the hopes, fears, frustrations, crises, potentialities. They succeed when events have prepared the way for them, when the community is awaiting to be aroused, when they can provide the clarifying and organizing ideas. Leadership completes the circuit between the individual and the mass and thereby alters history.

It may alter history for better or for worse. Leaders have been responsible for the most extravagant follies and most monstrous crimes that have beset suffering humanity. They have also been vital in such gains as humanity has made in individual freedom, religious and racial tolerance, social justice, and respect for human rights.

There is no sure way to tell in advance who is going to lead for good and who for evil. But a glance at the gallery of men and women in MODERN WORLD LEADERS suggests some useful tests.

One test is this: Do leaders lead by force or by persuasion? By command or by consent? Through most of history leadership was exercised by the divine right of authority. The duty of followers was to defer and to obey. "Theirs not to reason why/Theirs but to do and die." On occasion, as with the so-called enlightened despots of the eighteenth century in Europe, absolutist leadership was animated by humane purposes. More often, absolutism nourished the passion for domination, land, gold, and conquest and resulted in tyranny.

The great revolution of modern times has been the revolution of equality. "Perhaps no form of government," wrote the British historian James Bryce in his study of the United States, *The American Commonwealth,* "needs great leaders so much as democracy." The idea that all people should be equal in their legal condition has undermined the old structure of authority, hierarchy, and deference. The revolution of equality has had two contrary effects on the nature of leadership. For equality, as Alexis de Tocqueville pointed out in his great study *Democracy in America,* might mean equality in servitude as well as equality in freedom.

"I know of only two methods of establishing equality in the political world," Tocqueville wrote. "Rights must be given to every citizen, or none at all to anyone . . . save one, who is the master of all." There was no middle ground "between the sovereignty of all and the absolute power of one man." In his astonishing prediction of twentieth-century totalitarian dictatorship, Tocqueville explained how the revolution of equality could lead to the *Führerprinzip* and more terrible absolutism than the world had ever known.

But when rights are given to every citizen and the sovereignty of all is established, the problem of leadership takes a new form, becomes more exacting than ever before. It is easy to issue commands and enforce them by the rope and the stake, the concentration camp and the *gulag*. It is much harder to use argument and achievement to overcome opposition and win consent. The Founding Fathers of the United States understood the difficulty. They believed that history had given them the opportunity to decide, as Alexander Hamilton wrote in the first Federalist Paper, whether men are indeed capable of basing government on "reflection and choice, or whether they are forever destined to depend . . . on accident and force."

Government by reflection and choice called for a new style of leadership and a new quality of followership. It required leaders to be responsive to popular concerns, and it required followers to be active and informed participants in the process. Democracy does not eliminate emotion from politics; sometimes it fosters demagoguery; but it is confident that, as the greatest of democratic leaders put it, you cannot fool all of the people all of the time. It measures leadership by results and retires those who overreach or falter or fail.

It is true that in the long run despots are measured by results too. But they can postpone the day of judgment, sometimes indefinitely, and in the meantime they can do infinite harm. It is also true that democracy is no guarantee of virtue and intelligence in government, for the voice of the people is not necessarily the voice of God. But democracy, by assuring the right of opposition, offers built-in resistance to the evils inherent in absolutism. As the theologian Reinhold Niebuhr summed it up, "Man's capacity for justice makes democracy possible, but man's inclination to justice makes democracy necessary."

A second test for leadership is the end for which power is sought. When leaders have as their goal the supremacy of a master race or the promotion of totalitarian revolution or the acquisition and exploitation of colonies or the protection of greed and privilege or the preservation of personal power, it is likely that their leadership will do little to advance the cause of humanity. When their goal is the abolition of slavery, the liberation of women, the enlargement of opportunity for the poor and powerless, the extension of equal rights to racial minorities, the defense of the freedoms of expression and opposition, it is likely that their leadership will increase the sum of human liberty and welfare.

Leaders have done great harm to the world. They have also conferred great benefits. You will find both sorts in this series. Even "good" leaders must be regarded with a certain wariness. Leaders are not demigods; they put on their trousers one leg after another just like ordinary mortals. No leader is infallible, and every leader needs to be reminded of this at regular intervals. Irreverence irritates leaders but is their salvation. Unquestioning submission corrupts leaders and demeans followers. Making a cult of a leader is always a mistake. Fortunately hero worship generates its own antidote. "Every hero," said Emerson, "becomes a bore at last."

The single benefit the great leaders confer is to embolden the rest of us to live according to our own best selves, to be active, insistent, and resolute in affirming our own sense of things. For great leaders attest to the reality of human freedom against the supposed inevitabilities of history. And they attest to the wisdom and power that may lie within the most unlikely of us, which is why Abraham Lincoln remains the supreme example of great leadership. A great leader, said Emerson, exhibits new possibilities to all humanity. "We feed on genius. . . . Great men exist that there may be greater men."

Great leaders, in short, justify themselves by emancipating and empowering their followers. So humanity struggles to master its destiny, remembering with Alexis de Tocqueville: "It is true that around every man a fatal circle is traced beyond which he cannot pass; but within the wide verge of that circle he is powerful and free; as it is with man, so with communities." ●

CHAPTER

1

He Has Been Poisoned

ANYONE WHO HAD SEEN VIKTOR YUSHCHENKO'S BLOATED, POCKMARKED face knew that something was terribly wrong. He had been visibly ill for three months. Pictures comparing his current look to that of just a few months earlier had appeared on television and in newspapers worldwide. People speculated as to what had happened to him. On December 2004, the cause of his illness finally was confirmed. Viktor Yushchenko, opposition candidate for president of Ukraine, had been poisoned.

Like many people around the world, Dutch toxicologist Bram Brouwer had seen Yushchenko on television. He was startled by the transformation in Yushchenko's appearance. Brouwer contacted the Rudolfinerhaus Clinic in Vienna, Austria, where Yushchenko had been treated, and offered to test some of Yushchenko's blood for dioxins. According to Dr. Michael Zimpfer, director of the Rudolfinerhaus Clinic, those tests proved that Yushchenko's condition was the result of "high concentrations of dioxin, most likely orally administered."

On December 11, Austrian doctors confirmed that Yushchenko had indeed been poisoned with TCDD dioxin. Yushchenko's chief of staff Oleg Rybachuk suggested that the poison used was a mycotoxin called T-2. This Soviet-era substance, also known as Yellow Rain, was reportedly used during the Russian war in Afghanistan as a chemical weapon.

As defined by the Natural Resources Defense Council, dioxins are man-made chemical by-products. They are formed during the manufacturing of other chemicals and through incineration. Studies show that dioxins are the most potent man-made carcinogenic (cancer-causing substance) ever tested. They can cause severe weight loss, liver and kidney problems, birth defects, and death. As little as 5 milligrams (0.000176 ounce) of the substance can be lethal. Yushchenko's dioxin level was 6,000 times greater than what is normally found in the bloodstream. It was the second-highest level of dioxins ever recorded in a human.

In September 2004, Viktor Yushchenko had been in the middle of a hard-fought presidential campaign. His coalition party, Our Ukraine, was opposing the ruling party, the Party of Regions. Since gaining its independence from the Soviet Union in 1991, Ukraine had been ruled by people with close ties to Russia. These leaders were also known for their corruption and for their willingness to accept payoffs. Many had amassed large fortunes at the expense of the Ukrainian people.

These leaders were also known as ruthlessly authoritarian rulers. (*Authoritarian* indicates an organization or a state that embraces strong and sometimes aggressive measures against its own population. This is generally done without the consent of the people.) For the vast majority of Ukrainians, life under independence was no better than it had been under the harsh Soviet regime.

(Left) Viktor Yushchenko is photographed following his submission for candidacy in the Ukrainian presidential election on July 4, 2004. *(Right)* Yushchenko is seen at the Mariinsky Palace in Kiev on December 6, 2006, after suffering from severe Dioxin poisoning, which left his face disfigured.

Viktor Yushchenko promised to change all that. Fifty years old, handsome, and well-educated, with a beautiful wife and family, he was, in many ways, an ideal candidate for change. He had worked in the government, both as chair and governor of the National Bank of Ukraine and later as prime minister. When he was forced out of office by a no-confidence vote from his political enemies, he left office with his integrity intact. Yushchenko had earned a reputation as a clean and honest politician.

As the head of Our Ukraine, Yushchenko vowed that true democracy would bring a better quality of life to all Ukrainians. He vowed to establish closer economic and political ties with the West, with Europe and with the United States, and to

Yushchenko vowed that true democracy would bring a better quality of life to all Ukrainians.

pull away from Russia's influence. He hoped to gain Ukraine membership in the European Union and in NATO (the North American Treaty Organization).

Yushchenko's candidacy was a direct threat to the type of people who had ruled Ukraine for most of its history. If he was elected, the power of the oligarchs (groups of extremely powerful businessmen, who, in effect, ruled Ukraine, for their own gain) would be threatened. For them to remain in power, Viktor Yushchenko would have to be defeated.

As his wife, Kateryna, told CBS in a 2005 interview, "He was a great threat to the old system, where there was a great deal of corruption, where people were making millions if not billions [of dollars]," by their corruption.

On September 6, 2004, after a late dinner meeting, Viktor Yushchenko became ill. He began to vomit violently. He suffered extreme stomach pain and swollen organs. Doctors in Ukraine initially diagnosed it as a case of simple food poisoning, but other symptoms rapidly developed.

Yushchenko's face became paralyzed, and he was unable to speak or read. He also developed what is known as chloracne. This skin condition disfigured the face of the once moviestar–handsome Yushchenko, causing it to look puffy and scarred.

By September 9, it was clear to all that Yushchenko was suffering from more than just food poisoning. He was rushed to a clinic in Vienna, Austria, where doctors managed to save his life. He was diagnosed as having "acute pancreatitis, accompanied by interstitial edematous changes," a swelling of the liver, pancreas, and intestines. In addition, his digestive tract was covered in ulcers. This was said to be caused by "a serious

On September 18, 2004, presidential candidate Viktor Yushchenko addresses a crowd of approximately 15,000 supporters in downtown Kiev, just hours after being released from an Austrian hospital where he was diagnosed with Dioxin poisoning. In his speech, Yushchenko vowed to continue his run for presidency.

viral infection and chemical substances which are not normally found in food products." Yushchenko claimed that it was the work of government agents.

Even after treatment, Viktor Yushchenko was still a very sick man. With the first round of elections coming up on October 31, though, Yushchenko knew he could not stay out of the country for long. Only a week after arriving in Vienna, and barely recovered, he returned to Ukraine, eager to start campaigning again.

Throughout Ukraine, rumors spread rapidly about Yushchenko's medical condition. Even before the formal results of the tests were announced in December, it was assumed (at least by Yushchenko's supporters) that his political foes were behind the attempted murder. "Who did it?" "How did they do it?" and "Why did they do it?" were questions that would have to be investigated later. Right now, though, Yushchenko had an election to win. And, he knew that if his opponents were willing to stoop to murder, that there was nothing they would not do in order to win an election.

Little did Yushchenko know just how difficult the struggle would be. He could hardly imagine all the obstacles he and his allies would have to face. It would take three elections, one "Orange Revolution," and one decision by the Ukraine Supreme Court to ultimately resolve the election. Finally, however, the voice of the people was heard, and Viktor Yushchenko was elected by a wide majority to become the next president of Ukraine.

With Yushchenko's election, Ukraine reached a turning point in its history. It was a country that had never truly been free, and it had suffered much throughout its past. In the past century alone, it had seen Soviet domination, famine, purges, World War II, and political repression. Could Viktor Yushchenko live up to his campaign promises? Could he transform Ukraine? Could Ukraine shake off its past and become a successful, truly democratic society?

2

What Is Ukraine?

THE WORD "UKRAINA" CAN BE TRANSLATED AS MEANING "BORDERLAND" OR "on the edge." That, literally, is what Ukraine is. The country is in Eastern Europe, with Russia to the northeast, Belarus to the north, and Poland, Slovakia, and Hungary to the west. Romania and Moldova are on the southwest, and the Black Sea is to the south.

Except for the Carpathian Mountains in the west, the land is made up largely of fertile plains known as steppes. These flat, fertile areas have made Ukraine an important center for agriculture and an area ripe for conquest.

Throughout its history, the region has been wedged between powerful nations, which split the territory between themselves. Over the centuries, various nations have controlled the fate of the Ukrainian people: Russia and Poland from the mid-fifteenth century to the seventeenth, Russia and Austria throughout the nineteenth century, and Russia,

Poland, Czechoslovakia, and Romania during the twentieth. With the exception of a few very brief periods, Ukraine did not exist as an independent nation until after the collapse of the Soviet Empire in 1991.

Between the third and fifth centuries (A.D.), the Goths, Ostrogoths, and Huns took turns controlling the area. Slavic tribes, predominantly Bulgars, began to expand through much of Ukraine during the fifth century. They and other Slavic tribes spread through central and eastern Europe and into the Balkans in the sixth century. The descendants of this group became today's Russians, Ukrainians, Serbs, Poles, Czechs, and Bulgarians, among many others.

The ninth through the thirteenth centuries saw the rise of the state of Kievan Rus'. Its capital city was Kiev, which to this day is the capital of modern Ukraine. Curiously, Kievan Rus' was founded by neither Russians nor Ukrainians, but rather by Vikings. The Vikings were Scandinavians who also conquered parts of England and France. According to the earliest written history of the area, the *Tale of Bygone Years*, they had been invited into the region to bring stability to the local squabbling tribes. By the eleventh century, Kievan Rus' was, geographically at least, the largest state in Europe.

In A.D. 988, Grand Duke Volodymyr (*Vladimir*, in Russian) converted both himself and his empire to Christianity. Volodymyr had been a pagan who believed in many gods. According to the *Tale*, he decided that in order to "keep up" with the times, he needed to select a monotheistic religion. (Monotheism is the belief in one god.) So, he sent emissaries out to send him reports on the religions of the area.

According to Anna Reid in her book on Ukrainian history, *Borderland: A Journey Through the History of Ukraine*:

> The first people he consulted, according to the *Chronicle* [as the *Tale* is also known], were the Muslim Bulgars: "Volodymyr listened to them, for he was fond of women and

The Dnieper River, a major river that runs from north to south, partly serves as a natural border between Belarus and Ukraine. The river is an important asset to Ukrainian life, as it aids in the country's transportation and economy.

indulgence, regarding which he had heard with pleasure. But circumcision and abstinence from pork and wine were disagreeable to him: 'Drinking,' said he, 'is the joy of the Russes, and we cannot exist without that pleasure.'"

If Islam wasn't an option, Judaism or Catholicism didn't work for him, either. "We saw them performing many ceremonies in their temples," his emissaries reported back, "but we beheld no glory there." Glory, it turned out, was to be found in Constantinople, today known as Istanbul, the capital of Turkey.

In Constantinople, Volodymyr's representatives saw the Hagia Sophia ("The Church of Holy Wisdom"), at that time the Eastern Orthodox Basilica. Built by the Byzantine emperor Justinian I, it is considered one of the world's most beautiful buildings. It became an Islamic mosque in 1453, after the fall of Constantinople to the Ottoman Turks. In 1935, it was secularized and became the Asasofya Museum.

It was the city's role as the seat of the orthodox patriarch, though, that stunned the grand duke's emissaries:

> The Greeks led us to the edifices where they worship their God, and we knew not whether we were in heaven or earth. For on earth, there is no such splendor or beauty, and we are at a loss how to describe it. We only know that God dwells there among men and their service is fairer than the ceremonies of other nations.

It is for this reason that Eastern Orthodoxy (caused by the split of Christians in eastern Europe from the Roman Catholic Church in the west) became the religion of Kievan Rus'. Such decisions, seemingly made for unimportant reasons, can, as Anna Reid pointed out, change the course of history:

> It was one of the single most important events in the history of Europe. By choosing Christianity, rather than Islam, Volodymyr cast Rus's ambitions forever in Europe rather than in Asia, and by taking Christianity from Byzantium rather than Rome he bound the future Russians, Ukrainians and Belarussians together in Orthodoxy, fatally dividing them from their Catholic neighbors the Poles.

While it lasted, Kievan Rus', known to the rest of Europe as Ruthenia, was a civilization noted for its civility and sophistication. Bishop Gautier Saveraux of France reported that "this land is more unified, happier, stronger and more civilized than France herself." The laws were humane, and it is known that Anne, the daughter of Prince Yaroslav, was able to read and write (at that time, few women could do either)—much to the amazement of the French.

The Kievan Rus' Empire came to an end in the thirteenth century. The decline had begun a century earlier, when conflicts arose among the various principalities of Rus'. In 1237, the Mongols, led by Batu Khan, a grandson of Genghis Khan, crossed the Urals into Rus'. By 1240, Kiev had fallen to the Mongol hordes.

The Mongol army withdrew from Kiev two years later, leaving the city and much of the country in ruins. Foreign trade dried up. The city lost its religious status, as well, when the metropolitan, the senior churchman of Rus', moved his see, or capital, to the Russian city of Vladimir, and then to Moscow. The center of power was shifting to Russia.

The end of the Kievan Rus' Empire left unanswered questions between Ukraine and Russia. According to the Russians, the Kievan Rus' civilization moved to Moscow. The Russians saw themselves, not the Ukrainians, as the true heirs to the civilization. This has allowed them to ignore Ukrainian claims of independence, because they see Ukraine as part of a "Greater Russia." Ukrainians, of course, disagree. They see their civilization as separate from that of Russia. Two civilizations equal two separate nations. This difference in attitude continues today.

Northern and southern Rus' (today's Russia and Ukraine) were also separated by their treatment under the Mongols. Mongol troops left southern Rus' in a relatively short period of time. They made northern Rus' a part of their empire, though; it was known as the Golden Horde until the fifteenth century.

Many historians believe that the cruel treatment by the Asian Mongols changed the Russian people. They believe that it was from the Mongols that the Russians began their tradition of strong, despotic, and sometimes cruel leadership.

In the territory that became Ukraine, the principalities of Halych and Volodymyr-Volynsky emerged soon after the Mongol withdrawal. The two states eventually merged into a single state of Halych-Volodymyr. By the mid-fifteenth century, that state had fallen to Casimir IV of Poland.

Meanwhile, the "heartland" of Rus', including Kiev, was controlled by the Grand Duchy of Lithuania. Following the marriage of Poland's Queen Jadwiga to Lithuania's Grand Duke Wladyslav II Jagiello, most of the Ukrainian territories, with the exception of the eastern sections, were controlled by Lithuania.

The region underwent another change in control in 1569. Under the terms of the Union of Lubin, a significant part of Ukraine was placed under the control of the Polish crown. Poland was, and still is, a Catholic, not an Eastern Orthodox, nation. Under pressure from its new rulers, the Rutherian upper class converted to Catholicism as a way of gaining political influence. The vast majority of Ukrainians, especially the peasantry, remained faithful to tradition. They remained loyal to the Eastern Orthodox Church.

As the upper class became absorbed into Polish society, the gulf between them and the rest of the population continued to grow. In addition, Poland imposed serfdom on its subjects (wherein the peasantry was bound to the land and forced to work for the rich, upper-class landowners). Runaway serfs, and others, fled to the eastern border of the Polish-controlled territory and established what became a semiautonomous state. The people there became known as Cossacks.

As cowboys are to today's Americans, Cossacks are to Ukrainians. They are remote figures from the past, symbols of freedom and daring. The Cossack "state," known as Zaporozhian

Zaporozhian Cossacks emerged in the Ukraine as a result of changes to Poland's government and grew in numbers, creating conflicts to the rule of the Ottoman Empire. Cossacks based in Russia (shown above in 1919) became guardians of state and ethnic boundaries and were crucial members of the Russian army.

Sich, is considered by many Ukrainians to be the first true Ukrainian state. The region wasn't a state as we know it today, however. It had no physical boundaries or written laws. (It did have an open assembly known as the rada, however, where everyone had an equal voice.) It has been said that the Cossacks were not a people but were, rather, a way of life.

The Cossacks, hard drinkers and hard fighters, raided the surrounding territories in an effort to maintain their independence. They battled the Turks, who controlled the Tatars to the south. They fought the Commonwealth of Poland and Lithuania to the west. They also struggled against a Mongol-free and rapidly growing Muscovite Russia to the east.

In 1648, Bohdan Khmelnytsky led one of the largest uprisings against the Commonwealth of Poland and Lithuania. As Anna Reid pointed out in *Borderland*:

> Of all the endlessly mythologized figures of Ukrainian history, Khmelnytsky is both the most influential and the most mysterious. For Ukrainians, he is the leader of the first Ukrainian war of independence; for Poles he is the misguided peasant rebel who split the commonwealth…for Russians he is the founder of the Great Slav brotherhood, the Moses who led Ukraine out of Polish bondage into the welcoming arms of Muscovy.

For three years, Khmelnytsky was unstoppable. His troops seized control of all of present-day western and central Ukraine. After a series of military defeats by Poland, however, he decided that he needed an ally. He found one in Russia, and his decision proved to be a fateful one.

With the Treaty of Pereyaslav, signed in January of 1654, the Cossacks accepted Russian protection. The czar's title changed from "the autocrat of all Russia," to the "autocrat of all Great and Little Russia." (The czar was the head of Russia; the word derives from "Caesar" of Rome.) With that treaty, the destiny of Ukraine was signed over to Russia for nearly 350 years.

For the next 30 years, Polish, Russian, Tatar, and Cossack armies fought for control of the territory. When the dust settled in 1686, Kiev and all lands east of the Dnieper River

(Ukraine's major river, which runs roughly north to south, cutting the country neatly in half) were turned over to Russia. To the west, a weakened Poland soon disappeared from the map, as well, and by the mid-eighteenth century, western Ukraine (Galicia) was under the control of the Austrians. As the years passed, however, more and more Ukrainian territory fell under Russian control.

Throughout this period, the Ukrainians did their best to maintain their identity. The Russians, on the other hand, attempted to absorb Ukraine into Russia. Their goal was to make over the Ukrainian people as Russians. They actually went so far that in 1876, in the Edict of Ens, they banned the use of the Ukrainian language in publishing and education. All Ukrainian-language books were to be pulled from library shelves. Plays, concerts, and public lectures could only be presented in Russian. By controlling the language, the Russians felt they could control the citizenry as well.

Ukrainians resisted the czar's edict. As Reid described it in *Borderlands*, "In the villages, peasants took orders from their landlords in Russian, but still spoke Ukrainian among themselves."

World War I (1914–1918) was another turning point in the history of Ukraine. With the collapse of the Austrian Empire, and the successful Bolshevik (Communist) revolution in Russia, a Ukrainian nationalist movement emerged. Ukrainians felt that now was the time for them to achieve independence. They struggled to have their own nation, free from foreign domination.

During the years 1917 to 1920, several Ukrainian states emerged. The Central Rada, the Hetmanate, the Directorate, the Ukrainian People's Republic, and the West Ukrainian People's Republic all arose and just as quickly disappeared. In 1921, the Peace of Riga was signed between a reborn Poland and the Bolsheviks in Russia. It made all Ukrainian attempts at independence meaningless.

The Khmelnytsky Monument is located in central Kiev. A Cossak leader, Khmelnytsky led a successful uprising against Polish rule in the seventeenth century. Although it was intended to become an autonomous state, Ukraine later became annexed by Russia.

Once again, without the consent of the people living there, Ukraine was to be divided up. Galicia in the west was signed over to the Second Polish Republic. The majority of the country, the center and east, established as the Ukrainian Soviet Socialist Republic in March 1919, became a member of the USSR, the Union of Soviet Socialist Republics, in December 1922.

Ukraine's history to this point left its people without a sure sense of identity. Were they European, like the Poles, Austrians, and Lithuanians? Were they Russian? Reid pointed out that the Poles used to call western Ukraine "Eastern Little Poland" and the Russian name for Ukraine was "Little Russia." The Ukrainian spoken in western Ukraine contains a lot of Polish words. The language of central Ukraine is full of Russian words. Where does Ukraine fit?

Questions of this kind still hang over the Ukrainian people. It is only now, with independence, that answers can be determined. In 1922, though, the era of Soviet domination had just begun, and some of Ukraine's worst days were just ahead.

3

Soviet Domination

THE YEARS 1914–1921 HAD LEFT NEARLY 1.5 MILLION UKRAINIANS DEAD. The economy was in shambles. Ukrainians were desperate to rebuild their land. The early years of inclusion in the Soviet Union brought changes and revitalization to Ukraine and its people.

The Soviet leader Vladimir Lenin was eager to peacefully incorporate the country into the Soviet Union. To do so, he made many concessions to Ukraine. Economic growth among the peasantry and industrialization in the cities was encouraged.

The Bolsheviks were known for being antireligious. Despite this, however, two Ukrainian national Orthodox churches were created: The Ukrainian Autocephalous Orthodox Church (UAOC) and the Ukrainian Autonomous Orthodox Church. This was done for several reasons.

Above are the photographs of eight important members of the Bolshevik Party who played a vital role in the Russian Revolution. On the top row *(left to right)*, Vladimir Ilyich Lenin, Leon Trotsky, Joseph Stalin, and Karl Radek. On the bottom row *(left to right)*, Vyacheslav Mikhailovich Molotov, Roucharine, Lavrenti Pavlovich Beria, and Kirov.

One reason was to help the Soviets gain the support of Ukraine's peasant population. The two new churches were also created to break the power monopoly held by the old Russian Orthodox Church. That institution had been a mainstay of the prerevolution Russian Empire and was initially opposed to the new government. With government support, the new UAOC became very popular among the Ukrainian peasantry.

Perhaps even more important to the Ukrainian people was the new policy of korenization (indigenization). This policy encouraged the use of the Ukrainian language and led to a rebirth of Ukrainian culture.

Ukrainian-language schools were quickly opened through-out the country. This, in turn, raised the cultural level of the rural population. These newly literate people began to move into the cities, which rapidly became "Ukrainized" in both population and education. More books were published in the Ukrainian language, and the country's cultural life grew.

People were encouraged to speak Ukrainian at the workplace and in government. Initially, both the Communist Party and the government was mostly Russian and Russian speaking. By the end of the 1920s, however, ethnic Ukrainians made up more than half the membership of the Ukrainian Communist Party.

With the emergence of Joseph Stalin as the new leader of the Soviet Union (born in 1879 and ruled from the mid-1920s to 1953), the policy of Ukrainization came to an end. The newly confident educated elite Ukrainians had called for a move "Away from Moscow."

The Soviets responded to this movement with a clamp-down on liberties from 1929 to 1932, followed by an official end to Ukrainization in 1933. This Soviet reversal and attempt to break the growing nationalist movement coincided with per-haps the worst period in Ukraine's history—the Great Famine of 1932–1933.

Because of greater economic opportunities offered by the growth in industry, more and more Ukrainian peasants left the farms and moved to the cities. Ukraine was (and still is) a major agricultural center, however, and the Soviets needed grain supplies to feed both Ukraine and Russia. They also relied on the sale of surplus grain overseas as a source of income. In an attempt to increase production (as well as for other reasons that will be discussed later), Stalin ordered a collectivization of the state's farms.

Collectivizing the farms meant that all the peasants' land and animals were now to be owned by the state. The peasants themselves were forcibly brought together to work on the col-lective farms. On these farms, the land, animals, and crops were

Collective farms were created in Ukraine during the Stalin regime. The farms and everything on them, including the land, animals, and crops, were all controlled by the state. The photograph above was taken during lunchtime at Lenin's Way collective farm in 1936.

all owned by the state. As members of the collective, farmers were no longer working for themselves, but for the state itself.

A campaign began against so-called kulaks. Kulaks were supposedly well-to-do farmers. They were accused of opposing the regime and of withholding grain from the market for private use. Many were arrested, and whole "kulak" families were sent to concentration camps (the Gulag) and into exile in Siberia. The campaign against the kulaks was an excuse

By the end of the forced grain collections in March 1933, it is estimated that between 5 and 7 million Ukrainians had died of starvation.

for the government to arrest *anyone* who owned land and opposed collectivization.

Increased crop production quotas (the amount the state required the farmers to grow) were imposed on the farmers on the collective farms. The state ordered an increase in crop production of 42 percent in 1932 alone. These targets were unrealistic. Many historians believe that this was intentional.

On August 7, 1932, the government in Moscow imposed the death penalty in Ukraine for any theft of public property. Since all agricultural products were owned by the state, they were considered public property. Even the smallest amount of grain taken by peasants for their own use was considered theft.

Hundreds of starving Ukrainians died each month under the new law. If the farmers were unable to reach their grain quota, any other food was confiscated. Travel from the farming areas to other regions of Ukraine was banned, so people were unable to leave in search of food.

People who worked on the farms were not allowed any food until the quotas (which were impossible to reach) were met. Starvation spread. The work was enforced by both the army and secret police. Those who resisted were arrested and deported.

Conditions were unbelievably bad. People ate straw, weeds, leaves, tree bark, mice—anything they could to survive. Suicide, murder, and cannibalism were common. By the end of the forced grain collections in March 1933, it is estimated that between 5 and 7 million Ukrainians had died of starvation. It is estimated that an additional 6 million Ukrainians were "dekulakised," as well. Altogether, Ukraine lost somewhere between 25 percent and 50 percent of its rural population in a very short period. Since in many ways, the peasantry *was* Ukraine, the tragedy was felt for many, many years.

Why did it happen? Although some disagree, most historians believe that the Great Famine, or *Holdomor,* as Ukrainians know it, was no accident. They believe that it was a deliberate attempt by Stalin to destroy Ukrainian nationalism and culture.

What the Holdomor was to the countryside, the purges were to the cities. "Purges" in the Soviet system meant the removal, either through deportation to labor camps or by murder, of anyone considered an enemy of the state. Intellectuals, writers, artists—anyone who might question or resist Stalin's regime were arrested.

Anyone who was even heard saying something negative about Stalin or the regime could be turned over to the secret police. By the end of the 1930s, it is estimated that nearly four-fifths of the Ukrainian cultural elite had been eliminated. Even the Ukrainian Autocephalous Orthodox Church, created by the Soviets in 1922, was disbanded in 1930. Thousands of its priests were tortured, executed, or sent to labor camps in Siberia.

World War II began in Europe in 1939. Conditions in Ukraine were so bad at that time that, when the Nazis invaded in 1941, they were actually welcomed as liberators by many Ukrainians. Unfortunately, things were no better under the Nazis than they had been under the Soviets. If anything, things actually got worse.

The Nazis kept the much-hated collective farm system. In addition, they set to work carrying out their policy of genocide, or mass murder, against the Jewish population. They also deported Ukrainians to work as slave labor in Germany.

By the end of the war in 1945, the total civilian loss of life was estimated to be between 5 and 8 million people, including more than 500,000 Jews killed by the Einsatzgruppen, the

In the photograph above, refugees from Carpatho-Ukraine enter the north-western Romanian town of Sighet, after Hungarian troops occupied their homes. Carpatho-Ukraine briefly declared its independence in 1939 before it was occupied by Hungary, who then annexed the area in March of that same year.

"Special Action Squads" of the Nazi SS. Nearly one in six people had been killed.

After the war, the borders of Soviet Ukraine extended west. This finally united most Ukrainians under one political state. The war and the Soviet terrors preceding the war had left their mark, however. Ukraine was a shattered nation—its population decimated and survivors exhausted. Gradually, things began to improve. Agriculture began to recover, and Soviet industry, predominantly in the eastern sections of the nation, was slowly rebuilt.

Ukraine became part of the world community. It was part of the first group of nations to join the newly created United Nations. In 1954, the region of Crimea, which lies to the south of Ukraine, across the Black Sea from Turkey, was transferred from the Russian Soviet Federative Socialist Republic (RSFSR; today's Russia) to Ukraine. This was done to commemorate the three hundredth anniversary of the Treaty of Pereyaslav, the agreement that first opened Ukraine to Russian expansionism. It was into this world, nearly destroyed by war but slowly beginning to recover, that Viktor Yushchenko was born on February 23, 1954.

CHAPTER

4

Beginnings

VIKTOR ANDRIYOVYCH YUSHCHENKO WAS BORN IN THE SMALL VILLAGE OF Khoruzhivka, Sumy Oblast, Ukraine S.S.R. (An oblast is the equivalent of a province or state.) The village is located in the northwest of Ukraine, near the Russian border. It is, coincidentally, not far from the village birthplace of Leonid Kuchma, the man Yushchenko would replace as president of Ukraine in 2005.

Viktor's father, Andriyovych Yushchenko (1919–1992), served in the Red (Russian) Army during World War II. He was taken prisoner by the Germans but managed to escape from seven different camps. These camps, among the most brutal and deadly German concentration camps, included Auschwitz, Buchenwald, and Dachau.

The elder Yushchenko was also lucky to survive his return home after the war. Stalin suspiciously thought that being captured by the Germans was the same thing as surrendering to them. He distrusted anyone who spent time outside his control (even if it was in a prison camp). Many prisoners who returned home were shot, as possible "enemies of the state." Others were killed before they even arrived home. In many ways, Viktor Yushchenko was lucky to be born at all.

After his return to Khoruzhivka, the elder Yushchenko went to work as a teacher. He taught foreign languages, including English. It was at school that he met Viktor's mother, Varvara (Barbara) Tymofiyova (1918–2005). Varvara taught physics and math at the same school at which Andriyovych taught. They quickly fell in love and soon married. In addition to Viktor, they had one older son, named Petro.

As Andrew Wilson, author of *Ukraine's Orange Revolution* pointed out, it is important to emphasize that Viktor "is not from west Ukraine, the regions formerly under the Poland and the Hapsburg [Austrian] Empire, but from Sumy, which has been tied to Russia since the seventeenth century, some parts since 1503."

Viktor was born a country boy, in a small rural village. He speaks with an accent that includes *surzhyk* (the local mixed language of Ukrainian and Russian). He attended (and still attends) the Orthodox Church, which has close ties to Moscow.

Although his birthplace had long and close ties to Russia, Viktor grew up fully aware of Ukrainian history. From an early age, he was told about the Great Famine and the horrors that it brought upon his region. (Rural regions such as his suffered death rates as high as 15–20 percent of the population—400 people died in Yushchenko's tiny region alone.) He also learned about the village of Khoruzhivka's role as an outpost for Ukrainian Cossacks in the seventeenth and eighteenth centuries. Stories of their bravery inspired young Viktor's sense of Ukrainian patriotism.

As the son of schoolteachers, young Viktor grew up knowing the value and importance of education. He studied hard and excelled in school. He also had time for hobbies, including one rather unusual one—beekeeping. It is a hobby that he maintains to this day. As he describes it on his personal Web site, www.yushchenko.com.ua/eng:

> This hobby is rooted in my childhood. There was always a bee-garden at our place. My father, my grandfather, and my great-grand[father] took up the beekeeping. Since the early childhood, my brother and I have joined the adults to look after the bees and to listen to their lessons. My father used to say, "Bees' world is a unique community that has enough things in its stock to teach people. Hive is functioning according to the strict order, all duties are sharply defined: some bees stand guard over their hive, some of them bring the honey and others feed their babies."
>
> At present I have 80 bee families. I have both modern and rare ones from different parts of Ukraine in my bee-garden. It is situated in the country not far from Kyiv (Kiev). For summer I take my bees somewhere closer to bee plants. The most part of honey I give to the orphan asylums or give away to my friends. Beekeeping is the way of keeping the small part of that world where our ancestors used to live since it will never recur.

As a boy, Viktor was a romantic. He read, as he says on his Web site, "plenty of adventure books and there was a period when I was greatly impressed by Jack London's and Jules Verne's novels." Ukrainian poets and books of history were also among his favorites.

Teachers in small Ukrainian villages were not paid large salaries. Like teachers worldwide, those in Ukraine do not become teachers with the hope of getting rich. There was not a lot of money in the Yushchenko household for luxuries, so Viktor began earning money at an early age.

Seeing the sophisticated, well-dressed Yushchenko of today, it's easy to forget that as a boy he grew up in a small farm community. The following is a memory from his childhood, discussed in 2004, in an interview with Tetyana Kharchenko at http://www.artukraine.com. It paints an interesting picture of life for young Viktor. It also reveals that even at an early age he had an interest in banking and economics:

> Once I signed a contract with my grandmother Katrya, may she rest in peace. She gave me a task to graze three goats and said she would sell one of them in the autumn and give me money for it. I remember that I not only had to graze our neighbor's cows but also had to take care of those goats the whole summer. Grandmother Katrya did a fair thing, sold a goat and gave me all the money, as much as 28 rubles! That was my first serious financial project.
>
> At first I put that money in a cardboard box from vitamin pills and hid it at home inside the oven. Then every two to three hours I took the box out and recounted the money. In a while, I realized the oven was not a safe place, mother could find the money and spend it on things other than those I dreamt of. Therefore, I took those rubles out and hid them in a potato garden.
>
> Later I began to look for the money and could not find it. I kept searching for it the next day. In a word, I was not able to find the money. In September, when mother was digging the potatoes out, she came up to me and said: "I found your buried treasure yesterday. I spent it on a school uniform for you. That will be your present, Viktor." But how could that be a present?

You can imagine Viktor's disappointment. All that work, just for a school uniform. He understood, however, that a school uniform was more important than what he had hoped to buy—his own bicycle.

Sometimes Viktor was surprised by a gift that really was a gift. One of his fondest memories, also recounted in the interview on www.artukraine.com, is about a treasured gift he received from his older brother, Petro:

> I remember a football [soccer ball] which I got from him when I was 10. In the whole village nobody probably had a ball like mine. Even the school had only three balls, and one had to sign up to get a ball.
>
> So when Petro brought me my own ball, I even took it to bed with me when I was asleep. The ball had a nice new smell of leather. But it was not filled with air! As it turned out, pumping it required a special nipple pump. I asked all neighbors, searching for that pump, but nobody had it. Yet I was boundlessly happy with that present. It was something that I remember for the rest of my life.

Life in a small Ukrainian village was not easy. The Yushchenko family was comfortable, but not wealthy. In addition, as was the situation throughout the Soviet Union, food and manufactured products (such as air pumps) could be scarce or even unavailable. Nonetheless, Viktor had a happy childhood.

After finishing his primary education in Khoruzhivka, it was time for Viktor to go to university. He knew that he wanted to study accounting and economics, but he factored other things into his decision as to which school to attend. As he describes on his Web site:

> In my childhood, I was so much craving to see the mountains that this desire influenced my choice of the University in a way. One day the former students who were studying in Ternopil arrived at the school-leavers' [graduates'] party and told about wonderful landscapes of Galychyna, about the caves, Carpathians and age-old forests.
>
> In this way I made up my mind to enter the Ternopil Financial Economic University striving to devote myself

not only to learning but also to traveling. At the University, I joined simultaneously three study groups: speleology (the study of caves), mountaineering and tourism ones. At the same time I worked as an instructor for the mountain tourism.

I remember my first ascent of Hoveria [the highest mountain in Ukraine, 6,762 feet (10,882 kilometers), located in the Carpathians]. It was on the 22 of April in 1972, Lenin's birthday. [Vladimir Lenin was the head of the Bolshevik Party and the first premier of the Soviet Union after the Revolution of 1918.] And in three years in the same place, I got messed into the worst avalanche in my life. The route was carved just the next day and the group was able to descend.

Since that time there has arisen a tradition to go to the mountains with my friends once a year. And since 1990 when in July Verhovna Rada (Ukrainian Parliament) of that time passed the resolution about the sovereign state (Ukrainian independence) we have timed our annual ascent of Hoveria to this date. For me personally Hoveria is not just the highest peak of Carpathians but it's a symbol. In June of the year 2001 I declared about the foundation of "Our Ukraine" bloc there.

Viktor Yushchenko so loves the mountains that, with his doctor's approval, he climbed Mount Hoveria on July 16, 2005, less than a year after his near-fatal poisoning. Tragedy nearly struck again when Yushchenko and a group of his bodyguards were reportedly struck by lightning. The incident has never been officially confirmed. The media cited witnesses stating that Yushchenko and all but one of his guards were knocked unconscious by a lightning bolt. It has been confirmed, though, that other climbers were injured and killed by the same lightning strike.

Ternopil Finance and Economics Institute is located in the west of Ukraine. Yushchenko claims that his time there, in an area with far fewer historic associations with Russia than his birthplace, served to make him feel more "Ukrainian." He graduated from Ternopil in 1975 with a degree in accounting.

After a short stint as a deputy to the chief accountant at a kolkhoz, or collective farm, Viktor Yushchenko was called to serve in the military. Most young men in the Soviet Union served in the military when they turned 18, but Yushchenko was allowed to finish school first.

Yushchenko served as a conscript in the Border Guard unit of the KGB, the intelligence and internal security agency of the former Soviet Union. He was based on the Soviet-Turkish border. By coincidence, Viktor's birthday, February 23, was celebrated as Soviet Army Day. (It's now called Defender of the Fatherland Day.) As he described it in his interview with Tetyana Kharchenko on www.artukraine.com, the date has always had a great significance to him:

> When I was a child, I was very proud I was born on 23 February. I had a feeling as though I was not simply involved in a glorious function of being a defender and soldier, but also as though I was marked in a special way. When it was time to go to the army, I happened to serve on the border with Turkey. This was a very tough service, "full of deprivations," as our army newspapers put it.

Army life for a new conscript is never easy. Even though he'd grown up in the country, Yushchenko found it difficult. The conditions were rough and the work both boring and exhausting.

> I was conscripted in autumn. After our moderate climate, winters in the mountains of the Caucasus seemed harsh. In addition, I was four to five years older than all other conscripts, had a diploma and a job. So if for a lot of boys service was a test, regarded as a certain stage in maturing, I already looked at this in a different way.

The Bolsheviks founded the Red Army during the Russian Civil War in 1918. The photograph above was taken on February 23, 2003, as Russians march to celebrate Defender of the Fatherland day, a holiday that commemorates the birth of the Red Army. It is also Victor Yushchenko's birthday.

I can remember that initially I often asked experienced soldiers how long the service was. They said: "Viktor, this is all very simple: you come in the autumn, you are given a shovel. You keep shoveling snow until the shovel is taken from you, and that's when you know you have served half a term."

In the Caucasus, blizzards rage every day from autumn to spring. We did not even have water to wash our faces with, and had to melt snow to make tea. Yet drill annoyed more than everyday inconveniences. When soldiers are drilled senselessly, when you have to crawl with your overcoat on across heaps of snow ten times back and forth so that snow gets into your sleeves up to [your] armpits, you always begin to question the rationality of this kind of military service.

Yushchenko was not happy being away so far from home and missed his family and friends. The year was 1975, before cell phones and e-mail, and communication with loved ones was difficult at best. In an interview posted on www.artukraine. com/buildukraine/yushchenko23.htm, Yushchenko explained:

When you are in the army and get a letter from back home, this makes you feel very happy. Our frontier post was some 100KM from the closest settlement, [the Armenian town] of Leninakan, and Belarusian postman Tolya delivered mail once a week. That was quite an event, and we waited for Tolya as if he were the most important man.

Yushchenko's term of service ended in 1976. He was anxious to return to his career, to family and friends. Unfortunately, while Yushchenko was still in service on the border, he heard bad news about his girlfriend. In the same interview, he is quoted, "My friends wrote to me they had seen with her with another man. They told me to think hard and do something. I read this, but how could I get the attention of my beloved back when I was in the Caucasus? Time cured old memories, but back then it was not easy to bear this out."

Viktor Yushchenko left the military in 1976 and resumed his career in banking. For the next 10 years, his career grew slowly but steadily. His first major position was with the U.S.S.R. State Bank, located in Ulyanovsk, Russia. He worked there as an economist and department chief. In 1984, he received his graduate degree in finance and credit from the Ukrainian Institute of Economics and Agriculture. He returned home to Ukraine in 1985, where he was appointed Deputy Director for Agricultural Crediting for the Ukraine branch of the U.S.S.R. State Bank.

Public records of Yushchenko's private life are incomplete for this period. It is known that sometime in the late 1970s, or perhaps as late as 1980, he married his first wife, Svetlana Kolesnyk. They had two children: a daughter, Lina, and a son, Andriy. Viktor and Svetlana later divorced. It is alleged that some time after that Svetlana Kolesnyk killed herself.

In 1987, Viktor's career brought him to Kiev. There he met his first political patron, Vadym Hetman, at the U.S.S.R. Agroprombank. (A patron is a powerful friend who helps guide someone's career.) Some have alleged that family connections of Yushchenko's first wife helped him at this time, but others disagree. What cannot be disputed is that Yushchenko's career took off quickly.

As Yushchenko's career began to thrive, changes were happening throughout Ukraine, as well. After the end of World War II, the country became the center of the Soviet arms industry and high-tech research. Ukraine was also used by the Soviets as a major military and industrial outpost in its cold war with the West. Industries such as coal and iron ore mining, metallurgy, chemicals, and energy dominated the nation's economy. The products created by these industries were used in Ukraine, but largely by the military. As was the situation throughout Viktor's childhood, consumer goods throughout Ukraine were either unavailable or of poor quality.

In April 1986, a major explosion occurred at the Chernobyl nuclear power plant, in the Ukrainian town of Pripyat. The events at Chernobyl are described collectively as the worst accident in the history of nuclear power. After a steam explosion resulted in a fire, a series of additional explosions caused

Large areas of Ukraine, Belarus, and Russia were heavily contaminated by the radioactive fallout. More than 336,000 people were evacuated from the most heavily contaminated areas and resettled.

a nuclear meltdown, which released a plume of radioactive fallout from the plant.

The nuclear "cloud" drifted over parts of the western Soviet Union, eastern and western Europe, Scandinavia, the British Isles, and even eastern North America. Dozens were killed in the initial explosion, and it is estimated that thousands more will eventually die because of their exposure to radioactive material.

Large areas of Ukraine, Belarus, and Russia were heavily contaminated by the radioactive fallout. More than 336,000 people were evacuated from the most heavily contaminated areas and resettled. The long-term health dangers from radioactive material, such as cancer, rendered large areas of land surrounding the plant uninhabitable. Despite the disaster, the plant was not completely shut down until November 2000.

The Soviets experienced political fallout from the disaster, as well. The government tried to keep news of the explosion secret from the world. (In fact, it wasn't until nuclear power plant workers in Sweden were found to have radioactive materials on their clothing, which was determined *not* to be from the Swedish plant, that problems in the western Soviet Union were suspected.)

Soviet officials also responded slowly to the disaster itself. They did not notify Ukrainian citizens as to what had happened, or even start evacuations, until days after the accident. Ukrainians were outraged by the Soviet response. It seemed to them to demonstrate a complete lack of caring for the health

On April 26, 1986, an explosion at the Chernobyl nuclear power plant located near the Ukrainian city of the same name, released large amounts of radioactive material in the atmosphere, resulting in the worst nuclear catastrophe in history. The explosion at Chernobyl released 400 times more radioactive material in the air than the atomic bombing of Hiroshima, Japan.

and safety of the Ukrainian people. From these events, a new independence movement, called the Rukh, was born.

Changes were also occurring within Russia itself. Mikhail Gorbachev was now the leader of the Soviet Union. He introduced a policy of *perestroika* or "restructuring." Under perestroika, the traditional power of the Soviet state to run the economy was loosened, and private businesses were allowed to operate for the first time. This had an immediate effect on Yushchenko's career, when the local branches of U.S.S.R. Agroprombank were converted into a Ukrainian-run bank—Ukrainia—in November 1990. Yushchenko became the non-state-run bank's vice-chairperson, then first deputy chairman of the Republican Bank "Ukrainia."

With Gorbachev's policies of perestroika and glasnost, which encouraged a new openness and debate, independence movements rapidly grew throughout the Soviet Union. Events soon spun out of the Kremlin's control. (The Kremlin is the traditional seat of Soviet power, like the U.S. White House.) The Soviet Union quickly fell apart as one Soviet state after another declared its independence from Moscow.

Ukraine declared its independence on April 24, 1991. On December 1 of that year, Ukrainian voters overwhelmingly (90.3 percent) approved a referendum formalizing Ukraine's independence from the Soviet Union. That union formally ended on December 25, 1991. Ukraine's independence was officially recognized by the international community.

Independence did not necessarily equal democracy, however. The period 1991–2004 was marked by the presidencies of Leonid Kravchuk and Leonid Kuchma. Although Ukraine was supposedly independent from Russia, these men maintained extraordinarily close ties to Ukraine's former ruler. The people in power were former Communists. Despite a few changes in appearances, nothing had really changed for the vast majority of Ukrainians.

The period was also marked by harsh authoritarian rule and growing corruption. A few politicians and their business associates became extraordinarily rich at the expense of the Ukrainian people.

While Ukraine adjusted to its new independence, Viktor Yushchenko's career and personal life continued to be on the upswing. Vadym Hetman, Yushchenko's patron, who had become head of the National Bank of Ukraine (NBU) in 1991, resigned in 1993, claiming ill health. Before stepping down though, he made certain that Yushchenko, still relatively unknown, would be named his successor.

CHAPTER

5

Making a Name

VIKTOR YUSHCHENKO'S NEW POSITION AS HEAD OF THE NATIONAL BANK OF
Ukraine (NBU) turned out to be the right job at the right time.
Ukraine's economy was at the edge of disaster. According to
Anna Reid in *Borderland*:

> When the Soviet Union broke up, Ukraine was supposed to
> be the republic with the best chance of doing well economi-
> cally. Ukraine produced one-third of the Soviet Union's
> steel, nearly half of its iron ore, and half of its sugar. It was
> renowned for its fertile soil and agricultural development.
> According to a report from the World Bank, Ukraine could
> become one of the richest countries in the world.

> By 1993, however, Ukraine's economy was in shambles. The
> national currency, known as the coupon, had lost nearly all its
> value. Inflation was wiping out the nation's savings. Inflation

50

On September 2, 1996, the hryvnia *(above)* became the new Ukrainian currency. The hryvnia replaced the Karbovanets, an interim currency introduced in 1992 when Ukraine became an independent nation, as the official currency. As of November 2006, one U.S. dollar is equal to five Ukrainian hryvnia.

is, in economic terms, a rise in the price of goods and services. Some rise in prices is normal in a healthy economy. For example, in 2005, the United States Consumer Price Index, which tracks inflation, rose at an annual rate of 3.39 percent.

In Ukraine in 1993, the rate of inflation increased so rapidly that it became almost impossible to determine. Some had the rate of increase at 5,731 percent; others had it as high as 10,200 percent. People's life savings were made worthless. What

Ukraine's First Lady, Kateryna Yushchenko-Chumachenko, is a Ukrainian-American who was born and raised in Chicago. Kateryna met her future husband while working at a consulting firm in Kiev. Kateryna and Viktor Yushchenko have been married since 1998 and have three children together.

had once been enough money in the bank to live on for one's retirement was now barely enough to buy a pound of meat. Something had to be done.

Yushchenko took immediate action to steady the economy. By 1996, he'd brought the inflation rate down to 80.2 percent. By the following year, it had dropped to a nearly manageable 15.9 percent. In 1996, he also introduced a new currency into circulation, the hryvnia (UAH), which has proved remarkably stable. Yushchenko stayed at the NBU for six years—a remarkable success in a government where the typical minister lasted on the job for less then a year.

Also in 1993, Yushchenko met the woman who would become his second wife: Kateryna (Katherine) Chumachenko. Kateryna was born in the United States in Chicago, Illinois, on September 1, 1961. Her father, Mykhailo Chumachenko, and mother, Sofia, both were born in Ukraine. Mykhailo was one of the few members of his family to survive the Great Famine of 1932–1933. During World War II, Mykhailo served in the Red Army, was captured by the Germans, and was sent to a concentration camp. Sofia was sent to Nazi Germany as an Ostarbeiter (slave laborer from Eastern Europe). It was in Germany that they met and married.

At the war's end in 1945, Mykhailo Chumachenko became seriously ill with tuberculosis. He spent six years in a German tuberculosis sanitarium. In 1956, he received an invitation from the Ukrainian Orthodox Church in Chicago to emigrate there. Chicago was home to many displaced Ukrainians.

Kateryna Chumachenko was born an American citizen. However, her parents, like many Ukrainian immigrants, were anxious for her to grow up aware of her heritage. From early childhood on, she attended Ukrainian studies classes, as well as Ukrainian churches and youth groups. As a young adult, she became active in the Ukrainian human rights movement. She joined organizations that tried to bring attention to Ukraine's struggle for independence.

Chumachenko received her B.S. in International Economics from the Georgetown University School of Foreign Service in 1982. In 1986, she received her MBA, with a concentration in International Finance and Public Non-Profit Management, from the University of Chicago.

In 1982, Chumachenko secured a position as the Washington representative of the Ukrainian Congress Committee of America. There, she worked to inform the U.S. government, media, and non-government organizations (NGOs) about Ukraine. Beginning in 1986, with the United States Department of State, she helped write reports on human rights violations and researched religious suppression in the USSR. After two years at the State Department, Chumachenko moved over to the White House, where she became the administration's ethnic affair's liaison, organizing events for all Eastern European communities within the United States.

When she left the White House, Chumachenko worked at both the Treasury Department and for Congress, then served as cofounder and vice president of the U.S.-Ukraine Foundation. The foundation translated laws and texts for the newly independent Ukrainian parliament and government. In 1993, she joined KPMG Consulting, economic advisors to Ukraine, including the Central Bank. She moved to Kiev with KPMG, and it was there that she met Viktor Yushchenko.

Viktor and Kateryna married in a small church in January 1998. They have three children: two girls, Sophia and Chrystyna, and a son, Taras. Kateryna left her position with KPMG in 2000, when she was pregnant with their second child. Since then, she has devoted herself to her family and is active in charitable, historical, and cultural activities.

Having an attractive, well-educated, and accomplished wife, along with his own movie-star good looks, helped Viktor Yushchenko appear more worldly, sophisticated, and attractive than other Ukrainian politicians.

During the 1990s, Yushchenko's career had blossomed. He successfully managed Ukraine's economic crisis, which brought him international recognition as an economic reformer. He also fell in love and started a second family. Somehow, he also found time to continue his education. In 1998, he wrote his thesis, "The Development of Supply and Demand of Money in Ukraine," and successfully defended it, receiving his Candidate of Economic Sciences (Doctor of Economics) degree.

Life was good for Viktor Yushchenko. He was satisfied with his career and his life, but things were about to change. From his largely behind-the-scenes position as head of the NBU, he was about to move front and center into Ukraine's rough and tumble political system. In December 1999, President Leonid Kuchma unexpectedly nominated Viktor Yushchenko to be Ukraine's next prime minister.

6

In and Out of Government

WHAT'S THE DIFFERENCE BETWEEN A PRESIDENT AND A PRIME MINISTER?
Ukraine, like the United States, is a democracy. Its government has separate legislative, executive, and judicial branches. The president of Ukraine is, like the U.S. president, elected by a national popular vote. He or she is the head of the executive branch, is considered the head of state of Ukraine, and serves a five-year term of office.

Unlike the United States, however, Ukraine also has a prime minister. The prime minister presides over the Cabinet of Ministers (similar to the presidential cabinet in the United States). The Cabinet of Ministers is the top body of the executive branch of the Ukrainian government. The cabinet is made up of the prime minister, first vice prime minister, three vice prime ministers, and other ministers.

The prime minister is appointed by the president, and that person must then be approved by a majority vote of the

Verkhovna Rada (Ukraine's parliament). The prime minister manages the work of the Cabinet of Ministers of Ukraine and signs the acts of the Cabinet.

The prime minister is also responsible for carrying out the president's orders and directions. He or she can be dismissed from office by the president. In addition, the Verkhovna Rada can pass a resolution of "no-confidence" in the Cabinet, which must result in the prime minister's resignation.

Presidential elections were held in Ukraine in November of 1999. Leonid Kuchma was running for reelection. Many people in Ukraine were hoping that Yushchenko would run against Kuchma, who was considered an unpopular and corrupt president, with many dishonest allies. Yushchenko was reluctant to run. His longtime mentor, Vadym Hetman, had been murdered in 1998. This was considered by many to be a warning for Yushchenko himself not to get involved in presidential politics.

President Kuchma was still concerned that Viktor Yushchenko would challenge him for the presidency. According to journalist Kost Bondarenko, Kuchma and Yushchenko struck a deal. Yushchenko met with Oleksandr Volkov, a leading oligarch, as well as Kuchma's campaign manager. Volkov informed Yushchenko that it wasn't in Yushchenko's best interest to run for president at this time.

Volkov also told Yushchenko that if he declined to run and, instead, supported Kuchma in the election, that Kuchma would name him as Ukraine's next prime minister. Viktor Yushchenko did not run for president in 1999. Leonid Kuchma, allegedly with the assistance of electoral fraud and a few stuffed ballot boxes, won reelection.

On December 14, 1999, current Prime Minister Valerii Pustovoitenko lost his renomination vote by 206 votes to 44. President Kuchma then nominated Yushchenko, who won the Rada's approval 206 votes to 12.

Leonid Kuchma appointed Viktor Yushchenko as prime minister thinking that he would be able to control him and his

On October 31, 1999, Ukraine's second president, Leonid Kuchma, stands with his grandson, Roman, at a polling station in Kiev. Fearing competition from Yushchenko, Kuchma convinced him to take an appointment as prime minister instead of running for the presidency. During his presidency, Kuchma faced much scandal as he was implicated in the disappearance of a Ukrainian opposition journalist, Georgiy Gongadze, in 2000.

actions. Yushchenko had other ideas, however. He hoped to use his time in office and his position of prime minister to bring badly needed change to Ukraine. He hoped to bring about and support a true Ukrainian liberal movement. He also hoped to stop corruption and to create a true market economy.

Yushchenko knew, though, that he would have to take on the power of the oligarchs for any of this to happen. He was well aware that he would have to attack them before they could attack him. He appointed fellow reformer Yulia Tymoshenko as deputy premier in charge of the energy sector and got to work.

Yulia Tymoshenko was a sometime ally and sometime foe of Viktor Yushchenko. She did not start out life as a reformer. At age 19, she married Oleksandr Tymoshenko, the son of a midlevel Soviet Communist Party bureaucrat, and began to move up through the Soviet system.

Armed with the Ukrainian equivalent of a Ph.D. in economics, Tymoshenko founded a successful video retail chain. With Ukrainian independence, between 1990 and 1998, she began to direct several energy-related companies and earned a sizable fortune in the process. When Ukraine began privatizing (selling off state-run businesses to the private sector), her husband, by exporting metals, became one of the richest oligarchs in Ukraine.

From 1995 to 1997, Yulia Tymoshenko was president of United Energy Systems of Ukraine, a privately owned company that was the main importer of Russian gas in 1996. (Ukraine is almost wholly dependent on Russia for its oil and natural gas needs.) During that time, she was nicknamed "gas princess" because of accusations that she had stolen enormous quantities of Russian gas to sell abroad.

Despite her somewhat questionable beginnings, Tymoshenko moved into politics in 1996, running for Parliament and winning 91.1 percent of the vote in her home district. Noted for her good looks, expensive clothing, and distinctive hairstyle

Yulia Tymoshenko, shown here without her famous hairstyle, is a lead-ing Ukrainian politician. Tymoshenko was a major contributor in Viktor Yushchenko's success in the Orange Revolution and was appointed prime minister.

(one braid crowning the head, running from one ear to the other), Tymoshenko began positioning herself as a reformer and nationalist. She joined forces with Viktor Yushchenko in 1999.

Together, Viktor Yushchenko and Yulia Tymoshenko made a powerful team. Ukraine's dependence on Russia for natural gas and oil is a major economic and political problem for Ukraine, as is its ever-growing debt. The greater part of the problem, however, was caused by a plot between Russian and Ukrainian oligarchs.

As Andrew Wilson described the situation in *Ukraine's Orange Revolution*, most of Ukraine's gas came from the Russian company Itera, which was a front for the Russian gas giant Gazprom. In the mid-1990s, Gazprom was paying almost nothing for gas: around $4 per thousand cubic meters. Ukraine paid Itera about $50–$80, but Itera chose to receive only about a third of that. The balance, almost $2 billion a year for each side, was divided up between Ukrainian and Russian middlemen. Additional gas was sold to central Europe for $100–$110 per thousand cubic meters, generating another $360 million per year.

Tymoshenko allegedly profited from deals exactly like those in the past. Now, she moved to shut them down. As energy vice prime minister, she virtually ended many such corrupt arrangements in the energy sector. This brought much needed revenue to the Ukrainian government.

Progress was made along other fronts, as well. Collective farming was officially ended, and farmers were allowed to own their own land and crops once again. Because of this move, agricultural production nearly doubled between 1999 and 2004, which put additional food on the shelves. The increase in production also allowed Ukraine to once again export grain.

To pay off millions of dollars in Ukrainian debt, Yushchenko made cuts in federal spending. He also improved investment conditions in the country and overseas. Perhaps most

FOR YEARS, THE AVERAGE CITIZEN HAD LIVED IN FEAR OF THE GOVERNMENT; YUSHCHENKO WAS ABLE TO RESTORE PUBLIC TRUST IN THE UKRANIAN GOVERNMENT.

important, Yushchenko was able to restore public trust in the Ukrainian government. For years, the average citizen had lived in fear of the government: of its corruption and its ruthless government leaders who would stop at nothing to get what they wanted. Yushchenko hoped to restore honesty and open communication between the government and its people.

By 2001 though, Yushchenko's days as prime minister were numbered. The oligarchs were furious at his efforts to end their power and enforce the rule of law. As early as March 2000, President Kuchma would be heard on secret recordings saying, "I'll destroy Yushchenko," and adding "Yulia must be destroyed."

Yulia Tymoshenko was fired by President Kuchma in January 2001 on charges of forging customs documents and smuggling Russian gas while president of United Energy Systems of Ukraine. The following month, she was arrested and thrown in the notoriously squalid Lukianivskyi prison. After two months, Tymoshenko was released and cleared of all charges by one of Ukraine's few independent judges, Mykola Zamkovenko. Judge Zamkovenko herself was fired in July 2001.

Yushchenko was brought down by a no-confidence vote of 263–69 in Parliament, on April 26, 2001. The votes against him were from the oligarch's factions, the Communists (for a reported payoff of about $3 million dollars), as well as representatives of fake left-wingers and fake-nationalists. (Fake left-wing and nationalist parties were set up and funded by the authorities. In that way, voters would vote for a party thinking they were an opposition party, when they were actually a government party.)

It is not at all surprising that Yushchenko's government fell. His attempts at reform were a direct threat to the authorities and oligarchs who were becoming wealthy at the nation's expense. So, while the oligarchs were happy at Yushchenko's ouster, many ordinary Ukrainians were not.

More than 4 million voters signed a petition to bring Yushchenko back into office. Tens of thousands protested in Kiev. It was to no avail. He was out, and Kuchma's new man Anatoliy Kinakh was in place, to be replaced the following year by Viktor Yanukovych. The "old rule" government had survived Yushchenko's attempts at change, but just barely.

Things for the ruling authorities would never be the same. With both Yushchenko and Tymoshenko out of office, a reform movement was indeed possible. When asked in an interview when he decided to run for president, Yushchenko replied, "I would say the final decision was made on April 26, 2001."

Before the presidential elections of 2004, though, parliamentary elections were held in November 2002. Yushchenko ran as leader of the Our Ukraine (*Nasha Ukrayina*) political coalition. Our Ukraine was a moderate group, opposed to the Kuchma government. While he campaigned, Yushchenko emphasized his accomplishments while in office. He promised clean and honest government.

He also extensively discussed personal issues, such as faith and family values, and used images of his family in advertisements, as a selling point. Other opposition groups included the Socialists, led by Oleksandr Moroz, and Tymoshenko's own more radical bloc. It was called "Bloc of Yulia Tymoshenko" and had the initials BYuTy (pronounced "beauty").

Election night was a triumph for Yushchenko and the opposition. Our Ukraine won 23.6 percent of the vote, more than any other bloc. Tymoshenko's bloc won 7.3 percent of the vote, and the Socialists won 6.9 percent. The Communist vote

In 2001, Prime Minister Viktor Yushchenko answers questions during a news conference in Kiev. Yushchenko's reform policies were not well received by the opposition, and he was ultimately removed from office following a no-confidence vote by Parliament on April 26, 2001.

was 20 percent (down from 25 percent, just two years earlier). As for the two governing parties, For a United Ukraine won a mere 11.8 percent, and the Social Democratic Party of Ukraine (United) only 6.3 percent.

Only half of the seats in the Rada were won by popular vote. The other half were elected by smaller bodies within each district. It was here that the government, old-line politicians and oligarchs, were able to take charge. Of those extra 225 seats, the opposition won only 54, and the Communists only 7.

The authorities, on the other hand, won 161 seats. With those 161 seats, plus extra votes won by a combination of pressure and bribery, the authorities managed to gain majority control of the Rada. Outmaneuvered and outspent, the opposition had to settle for being a strong, though powerless, minority.

Despite their ultimate loss, the opposition had achieved a symbolic victory—a major psychological breakthrough. They showed that, after 10 years of rule by the same corrupt group, there was a real opposition movement in Ukraine. From their victory in the popular vote, they showed that the authorities were vulnerable.

The government learned a slightly different lesson. They realized how close they had actually come to losing control of Parliament. They knew that the only way to win the upcoming presidential elections of 2004 was to do everything necessary— legal or illegal—to keep Viktor Yushchenko and the opposition out of office.

CHAPTER

7

Our
Ukraine

THE THREE MAJOR PLAYERS IN THE DRAMATIC PRESIDENTIAL ELECTIONS
of 2004 were Viktor Yushchenko, Yulia Tymoshenko, and
the man who was then Ukraine's prime minister, Viktor
Yanukovych. Yushchenko was the great hope of the common
people in Ukraine politics: He had a clean and honest image
and was also admired by the West. On the negative side,
Yushchenko was sometimes criticized for being indecisive and
was accused of being unable to form a unified team capable
of working together.

Despite the negatives, Yushchenko was the first real chal-
lenger to the Ukrainian government to come from *within* the
system. Because of this, he knew its strengths and weaknesses.
Unlike previous opposition candidates, he was enough of an
insider to defeat the former Soviet elite at their own game.

It was no secret in Ukraine that although elections were
held, no opposition candidate would ever be allowed to win

the presidency. People had given up hope that someone would be able to beat the system. Viktor Yushchenko changed that. When he made his official announcement that he would seek the presidency, he brought hope to millions of Ukrainians who wanted change.

Yulia Tymoshenko also knew all aspects of the system. Becoming rich by trading gas and oil, she switched sides at the right moment and joined the opposition. She was extremely tough (tougher and more decisive than Yushchenko) and knew all the tricks that the regime used to stay in power.

But who was Viktor Yanukovych? Born on July 9, 1950, Yanukovych was orphaned by the time he was a teenager and was thereafter raised by his grandmother. Twice, in 1968 and 1970, he was convicted and imprisoned on charges of robbery and causing bodily injury. According to Yanukovych, his record was cleared in 1978, but no documentation has ever been presented to back up his claims.

After leaving prison, Yanukovych held down various jobs, which included working as a car mechanic. He finally was promoted to a position in which he looked after cars at the Ordzhonikidze Coal Production Association. In 1980, he graduated, by correspondence, from the Donetsk Polytechnic Institute with a major in mechanical engineering.

Like Viktor Yushchenko, Viktor Yanukovych's career began to thrive once he found the right patron. His patron was former Russian cosmonaut Georgii Beregovoi, who had spent four days in space in 1968. With his help, Yanukovych's old convictions were supposedly cleared up, and he received his membership card in the Communist Party. This was the beginning of his management career in regional automotive transport.

Yanukovych's political career began when he was appointed a vice head of Donetsk Oblast Administration in August 1996. He quickly moved up the political ladder, becoming prime minister of Ukraine on November 21, 2002. He also received a degree from the Ukrainian Academy of Foreign Trade as a master of international law in 2001.

Despite his degrees, the publication of documents hand-written by Yanukovych revealed numerous spelling mistakes. They showed that he was unable to properly write his position or even his wife's name in Ukrainian. (Like many people who grew up in eastern Ukraine, which is more Russian than the more Ukrainian west of the country, Yanukovych grew up speaking Russian.) Because of this, he was mocked in the media and questions were raised about his professional abilities.

Yanukovych has also been accused by his political opponents of having close ties to organized crime. He is closely linked to the clan of Donetsk, an eastern-Ukrainian-based business and political group. It is headed by oligarch Rinat Akhmetov.

Since 2002, Viktor Yushchenko had been leading in all presidential polls, with between 23 percent and 26 percent of the vote. These were roughly the same percentages that Our Ukraine had garnered in the 2002 parliamentary elections. On July 2, 2004, Yulia Tymoshenko announced that she would not run for election herself. Instead, she threw her support behind Yushchenko. Two days later, on July 4, Viktor Yushchenko declared himself a candidate for the presidency of the Ukraine. With Tymoshenko's support, new polls showed him well in the lead, with more than 30 percent of the vote.

Why did Tymoshenko decide not to run? It was a matter of self-preservation. Since the time of her arrest and jailing in 2001, the Kuchma regime had done everything in its power to destroy her. She knew that her only chance of survival was if the regime itself was defeated. She calculated that Yushchenko had the best of change of getting that done. Under the banner "Force of the People," she declared her unity with him.

Faced with Yushchenko's growing popularity in the polls, the authorities tried everything they could think of to defeat him. Most plans included changing election practices: At one point, they considered canceling the elections altogether. One

Viktor Yanukovych is photographed at a 2004 presidential rally in Kharkiv, Ukraine. After serving as prime minister of Ukraine from 2002 to 2004, Yanukovych ran against Viktor Yushchenko in the controversial 2004 presidential election.

Faced with Yushchenko's growing popularity in the polls, the authorities tried everything they could think of to defeat him.

plan would have delayed the presidential election until after the parliamentary elections of 2006. Another was for the Rada, not the people, to choose the next president.

A third plan was to have the 2004 and 2006 elections go on as planned, but with a change. The 2006 parliament would be elected to a five-year term and would select a new president in 2006, which would greatly shorten the term for whomever was elected to that position in 2004. Despite tremendous pressure and alleged falsifying of votes, this last plan was defeated in the Rada, just six votes short of gaining the majority needed for victory.

A second option was to create a "strategy of tension," or "organized chaos." It was hoped that this would intimidate some voters and pressure others into supporting Yanukovych. These attempts, a few scattered bombings, fake riots, and stolen ballot boxes in local elections did not amount to much.

A third and more successful option was to reposition Yanukovych as a populist. Ads tried to create an image of Yanukovych as being an oppositionist candidate. As such, he spoke about "old power" (Kuchma) vs. "new power" (himself).

The government sprang to his aid. They gave his candidacy a huge boost by awarding a large increase in the state pension for the elderly. This pension was doubled in September 2004, from UAH137 to UAH284 (about $54.00). The move proved effective, and Yanukovych moved ahead in the polls by 10 points between mid-September and mid-October.

This lead proved temporary, though. The increased pensions helped push inflation up and the exchange rate down. This jolt to the economy stirred fears of a return to the hyperinflation of the 1990s, and Yanukovych's numbers in the polls soon returned to their previous levels.

The authorities' fourth option was to play on the country's long-term east/west split. As discussed earlier, the eastern and southern sections of Ukraine were, in many ways, more Russian than Ukrainian. The authorities hoped to stir the fears of the eastern, or Russian, half of the country that it could lose its identity to the western "Ukrainian" side.

So, on September 27, 2004, Yanukovych made a public commitment to make Russian an official language. (Ukrainian has been the only official language in Ukraine since independence in 2001.) He promised to allow Ukrainians to hold citizenship in both Ukraine and Russia. He also vowed that Ukraine would not join NATO. These moves were a blatant attempt to gain votes among the Russian-speaking Ukrainians of the cities of the east and south.

Russia did its part to assist Yanukovych's campaign, as well. Money was poured into his election coffers, and Russian political consultants were brought in to help him get elected. Russia dropped the VAT (value-added tax) from the cost of oil exports to Ukraine, making the price 16 percent cheaper.

Russian president Vladimir Putin also got involved. In support of Yanukovych, he made many high-profile visits to Ukraine, including a 90-minute phone-in broadcast on official Ukrainian television. Obviously, the Russians were desperate to keep Yushchenko from getting elected. He vowed to move Ukraine away from Russian influence and toward Europe and the United States. It was in the Russians' interest to keep Ukraine under its influence.

The authorities also tried to scare off Russian-speaking voters. They did this by trying to paint Yushchenko as an extreme Ukrainian nationalist. This was untrue—he was running to be president of all Ukrainians, not just the Ukrainian west. That didn't stop the government's propaganda campaign, however.

On August 2, 2004, as a presidential hopeful, Viktor Yushchenko *(right)*, stands with socialist leader Oleksandr Moroz, after signing an agreement for a fair presidential election.

The authorities hired four "fake" nationalists to run for president and used them to make Yushchenko look bad. One of the four, Roman Kozak, ran ads on television saying, "Vote for Yushchenko. Together . . . we will kick the Russians and Jews out of Ukraine." This was not what Viktor Yushchenko stood for, and the voters knew it. The four "fake" candidates together pulled in only 0.35 percent of the vote.

In their desperation, the authorities also tried to link Yushchenko with U.S. president George W. Bush, who was running for reelection at the same time. Ads referred to him as "Viktor Bushchenko." As Andrew Wilson described the situation in *Ukraine's Orange Revolution*, posters appeared of George W. Bush peeking out from a Yushchenko mask and saying, "Yes! Yushchenko is Our President!"

Another poster appeared, showing a mosquito, in the colors of the stars and stripes, sucking Ukraine's blood. Another particularly vicious poster showed Ukraine divided into three parts: the first-class west Ukrainians and the second-class central Ukrainians discriminating against third-class citizens in the east and south.

Yushchenko was viciously attacked for leaving his first, "proper Ukrainian" wife, Svetlana. His opponents were not content attacking the candidate himself; they also went after his wife, Kateryna. As far back as 2001, the Russian government TV station ORT broadcast a program called "Odanko." In it, it was claimed that Kateryna Yushchenko was an American spy who worked for Zbigniew Brzezinski (former National Security Advisor to President Jimmy Carter).

It was said that Kateryna had been sent to Ukraine to meet Viktor Yushchenko and to help bring him to power. The show also claimed that Yushchenko had been a nobody until his wife came along—that he was nothing but a "tool" of American interests. The show was later rebroadcast on Ukrainian television.

In an interview with Waldemar Piasecki posted on www. brama.com, Yushchenko laughed at the possibility of his wife influencing him politically or professionally, saying, "Any woman, even the most powerful one, that has three small children on her hands can only be concerned with household problems. There is no time or energy left for anything else. I have a beautiful wife who is truly the guardian of our home, where we have a wonderful family atmosphere, which allows me to rest and forget about politics."

Kateryna sued the station for libel and won. The court said that the accusations were not true and fined the stations for broadcasting the slander. Accusations like these were still made against her throughout the campaign, however.

Through it all, Viktor kept campaigning. He was certain that he offered the best opportunity for a new Ukraine. Again and again, he promised to end corruption. He promised closer ties with the United States and Europe. He promised to unite all Ukrainians, east and west, to build a better future for all. He spoke, as Andrew Wilson put it, "of dignity, of moral values in government, and of respect for the citizen in a way that Yanukovych could not."

Because the media was controlled by the government, Yushchenko was unable to get equal time or fair coverage in radio, television, or newspapers. He was forced to bring his campaign directly to the people. He worked tirelessly, traveling throughout Ukraine. He addressed voters in big cities and tiny villages, going anywhere he could, to get his message of hope and change to the public.

The public responded. Despite everything the entrenched authorities could throw at Viktor Yushchenko, he would not be defeated. As he stated in an interview posted on his Web site,

> I made a statement saying that I had made my choice and that I would seek the presidency in front of 70,000 people who came to Spivoche Pole in Kiev on July 4 from literally all cities and towns of the country. This is my conscious and final choice. Millions of people support me, they trust in me. I must go and I will go all the way through for the sake of

our common victory. I will say to those who hope that I will drop out of the race: Not on your life.

The authorities had one more card up their sleeve. On September 5, 2004, Viktor Yushchenko had a secret dinner with the head of the SBU (the Ukrainian Security Service), Ihor Smeshko, his deputy Volodymyr Satisuk, and Our Ukraine supporter David Zhvania. The meeting was held at Satsiuk's dacha (estate), outside Kiev. Yushchenko's goal in going to the meeting was to try to persuade the SBU to follow the constitution when it came to the presidential elections.

The meeting was held from 10:00 P.M. to 2:45 A.M. The four men dined on boiled crawfish, beer, salad, vodka with meats, and an after-dinner cognac. The food was all prepared by Satsiuk's private chef. Yushchenko went home immediately after the dinner. According to one account, Yushchenko vomited on his way home, which may have saved his life: He would have expelled up much of the poison. In an interview posted on her husband's Web site afterward, Kateryna recalled what happened when her husband returned home:

> Of course, I have always feared for Viktor, but I never imagined that his enemies would carry it this far. That is why the first symptoms of his illness did not cause me serious concern. I remember the evening very well. On (that night) Viktor came home late. I, as usual, kissed him and felt a strange taste of medicine on his lips. I even asked him if he took any medicine. Viktor said he did not. He said he was tired and said that he did not really want to go to that last meeting.
>
> At first I tried to reassure myself, thinking that it was just an ordinary illness that anybody could have. Moreover, until the Ukrainian doctors diagnosed food poisoning, we thought it was just weariness, result[ing] from his endless tours, rallies and meetings with people.

HE SUFFERED EXHAUSTION, EXTREME PAIN, AND SWELLING. HIS FACE BECAME SWOLLEN, AND LESIONS AND POCKMARKS APPEARED ON HIS FACE AND BODY.

The next day, Ukrainian doctors diagnosed Yushchenko's illness as food poisoning. Over the next several days, however, instead of getting better, his condition steadily worsened. He suffered exhaustion, extreme pain, and swelling. His face became swollen, and lesions and pockmarks appeared on his face and body. On September 9, Yushchenko left Ukraine for the Rudolfinerhaus Clinic in Vienna, Austria. As Kateryna recalled:

> [We] understood how serious it was only a few days later, when my husband felt worse. Some of our friends and my husband's colleagues insisted on an urgent examination in a reputed European hospital from the very outset. They talked about the need for an independent examination, and about security issues. But we hesitated to make the decision. Fortunately, the decision turned out to be correct, since, according to the Austrian doctors, the preliminary diagnosis made here, in Ukraine, and the treatment prescribed were inaccurate. So by delaying the hospitalization we ran the risk of losing Viktor. Doctors believe that had we been only a few days later there was an 80 percent chance that he might have died.

The attempted murder of Viktor Yushchenko was much more than just another ugly moment in Ukrainian politics. It was also a near tragedy for the Yushchenko family. Yushchenko's mother had suffered a heart attack a few days prior to the poisoning. Her family would not let her watch the news on Ukrainian television.

Like any mother, Kateryna tried to downplay the serious of Viktor's condition to their children, at least until he returned home from Austria. His oldest children, Vitalina and Andriy, took the news very hard. The two younger ones, Sofia and Crystyna, were too young to fully understand what was happening. Like any young children, they continued to ask what was wrong with their father.

It was the love and support of Kateryna and his youngest child, Taras, though, that helped Yushchenko get through the darkest days in the Austrian clinic. As Yushchenko described later to interviewer Waldemar Piasecki:

> My family has become my greatest source of strength after becoming ill. Kateryna along with our seven-month-old son Taras did not leave my side in the Austrian clinic. Taras alone, without realizing it, aided me with just his presence and good humor. At the hospital, his first tooth started growing in and he started sitting up. I thank God and value every minute that I can spend with my children, mother and wife.

When he returned to Ukraine from Vienna on September 18, Viktor Yushchenko addressed a waiting crowd of tens of thousands of people gathered in European Square. Exhausted, his face swollen and covered with sores, he told the crowd, "My dear Ukrainians! I am happier than ever to be here today with you!" Despite his still serious medical condition, the campaign would continue.

An initial report from the Austrian clinic claimed that no evidence of poison had been found. This report, later proved to be a fake, was possibly linked to oligarch Viktor Pinchuk. But the fake report was all that the official Ukrainian media needed to hear.

Newspaper articles claimed that he looked the way he did because he had a bad hangover. It was said that his illness was caused by a botched botox injection. It was even said that he had herpes. The majority of Ukrainians did not believe those wild claims. They could see with their own eyes how ill Yushchenko had been and how much his appearance had changed.

Deep in their hearts, too, Ukrainians knew that their government was perfectly capable of attempting to kill Viktor Yushchenko or anyone else, for that matter, if that's what it would take for them to win an election. It wasn't until December 10 that Yushchenko's attempted murder by dioxin poisoning was confirmed by medical authorities. An attempt *had* been made on his life.

How did Yushchenko respond to the attack and to his painfully altered appearance? Nearly a year after the attack, he tried to explain to Larry King, in an interview posted on Yushchenko's Web site.

> Well, first, it's very difficult because I got used to seeing such Yushchenko every day in the mirror every morning. The most painful thing for me was how my children perceived this, how my family perceived this. Because children, you know, they do not know any diplomatic language and sometimes they can tell you directly what they think. But I'm really grateful to them for accepting me the way I am. It's not—I'm not in the best shape of course, and—but the time will go by and I'm just pretty sure that I will completely recover from that. I will find a way from the cycle of this illness, of this disease because some stages of the program of recovery—the program of treatment and there are some specific terms when some of the inflammation process will be stopped and then I will be able to say that there is some kind of improvement on my face.
>
> But it just—I had to—we just need to understand one thing, that poisoning is not a simple flu. It's not like you wake up tomorrow and you are absolutely different, because you will remain the same the day after tomorrow and so on

and so forth. Probably then, in the future, you will get your initial look, but it takes time.

I'm very happy that God didn't take anything from me, neither my mind neither my force. You know, when I was in hospital, in all churches of Ukraine people prayed for my recovery. And you know, I just can't imagine how much I should pay to those people, how long I should stay on my knees [in prayer] in order to pay the tribute to all their voices and efforts.

Like any wife, after the attempted murder, Kateryna was terrified that the authorities might try to kill her husband again. Yushchenko could easily have returned to the private sector and had a successful career in banking or business. Did Kateryna ever try to get him to leave politics? As she says on Viktor Yushchenko's Web site:

I would be lying if I said that I did not try. Of course I tried to talk to him about his security, about our children and about the most important thing for us, that he be always with us. Viktor is indeed a highly educated and highly professional economist and he would always find a good job. But all of these talks were nipped in the vine. First, it is impossible to influence Viktor, even if it is a domestic matter.

Second, he insists that we do not talk about politics at home. And the most important thing is that his decision to go into politics was prompted by only one wish, to serve Ukraine. This is the cause of his life, and believe me, I do not want to say fine words, but for the last several years his work has been dedicated to only one goal. He sincerely wants Ukraine to be a prosperous and democratic country.

[Besides] he knows what Ukrainian politics is like, and he does not have any illusions about the presidential campaign. The problem is that Viktor never complains: He keeps all his pain, moral and physical, inside himself. He tries to safeguard his family from any troubles. With respect to this situation, he reassured us, saying that we got off lightly. He is optimistic and he never concentrates on the negative. Viktor is a believer and he is convinced that God and the support of his family helped him to survive.

I know it is easier for Viktor when we [his wife and children] are near. Now, when he has dozens of meetings every day, when he talks to thousands of Ukrainians, he needs a special, comfortable and warm atmosphere at home. He wants to see his family and to feel our support. Of course he misses contact with the kids. That is why he spoils them and says that I am a strict mother!

Government officials went into Election Day, October 31, 2004, confident of victory. The government-controlled media was on their side. All the power of the government was on their side. How could they lose? What they failed to count on was the sincere desire of the Ukrainian people for change.

Exit polls are surveys of voters taken after they have left the polling booth; these polls ask the voters who they supported in the election. Taken accurately, exit polls are a highly reliable way of forecasting the results of the election. When government authorities and Yanukovych campaign workers saw the first exit polls, they were stunned. Viktor Yushchenko was leading Viktor Yanukovych by 44.8 percent to 38.1 percent. This was unacceptable. Something would have to be done.

Electoral fraud had always been part of the government's plan to win. Traditional fraudulent methods included collecting votes from people who were dead, but were still registered to vote, fake ballots, and transportation of paid voters by bus and train from one polling place to another for repeat voting. (It is estimated that between 1.5 and 2 million fraudulent votes were cast through this system alone.)

In addition, in areas of the country where Yushchenko had particularly strong support, in the west and center, voters might

On October 31, 2004, Viktor Yushchenko exits a polling booth with his daughter, Khrystyna, in Kiev, the Ukrainian capitol. The 2004 presidential race called for three rounds of voting, due to reports of electoral fraud.

appear at their polling place, only to learn that a mistake had been made, that they weren't on the voter's roll, and "sorry," they would not be allowed to vote.

Another way the government manipulated the vote count was through absentee ballots. These ballots were sent by mail by the elderly and sick—people unable to come to the polling stations themselves. The percentage of absentee ballots in areas of Yanukovych strength was absurdly high—in some polling stations, more than 30 percent of the voting was done by absentee voters. Of course, there was no way that one in three voters was too old or sick to physically vote, but absentee ballots are the easiest to fake or manipulate.

All these tried and true techniques were in place and used on Election Day. New times called for new measures, however. Yanukovych had a special team of computer experts set up in case of election emergencies. The team was linked by fiber-optic cables to the Central Election Commission (CEC).

The computer experts were able to intercept local vote counts as they were sent electronically to the CEC, manipulate the results, and then send them on to the CEC. It was a fairly foolproof system, although mistakes were made. According to Andrew Wilson, on the CEC's Web site, in seven regions, more votes were recorded electronically than there were paper ballots handed out—129,956 in total.

Still, the authorities had been overconfident. Despite all their efforts, they had done too little, too late. Even after the vote count was stopped twice, in an effort to manipulate the count, when the final results were announced on November 10, Yushchenko came in first, but by only 39.9 percent to Yanukovych's 39.3 percent. Because neither candidate had gained a majority of the vote, a runoff election would have to be held on November 21. This time, though, the authorities would be ready.

8

End of Politics as Usual

TIME BEFORE THE RUN-OFF ELECTION ON NOVEMBER 21 WAS LIMITED, AND Viktor Yushchenko was eager to hit the campaign trail. As he discussed in an interview with Waldemar Piasecki at www. brama.com:

> I intend to live and work not only until the elections, but also beyond them—in order that a democratic and affluent Ukraine becomes a reality. As you see, the attempt to remove me during the pre-election stage failed—I survived, and now I am filled with renewed energy and determination even more than before. My health has returned to normal. As of October 10, I actively rejoined the election campaign, and within three weeks visited twelve regions of Ukraine and met with tens of thousands of voters. Although the attack on me was severe, and I would prefer to feel even better than I do now, I survived—thanks to the support of my family, friends,

and millions of Ukrainians who wished me well. I am sure that we will find out . . . why someone tried to remove the leading candidate during the most active phase of the race for president. But the plan failed. And I fear nothing. I am prepared to pay any amount for the sake of one thing—for Ukraine's future.

On Election Day, the exit polls indicated a victory for Viktor Yushchenko. The most reliable of the polls, the KISS-Razumkov poll, showed him leading Yanukovych 53.7 percent to 43.3 percent. Even more biased polls, such as the "People's Choice" poll done by the SOCIS Center for Social and Political Investigations and by Social Monitoring, had Yushchenko ahead of Yanukovych by 6.4 percent.

When the authorities and Yanukovych campaign officials saw those figures, they knew that their usual forms of electoral fraud would not work. The Zoriany (a secret team of computer experts working for Yanukovych, who were housed in the Zoriany movie theater) would have to move into action. The results were readily apparent. Although during the first round of voting, the count took nearly two weeks, in the second round, a winner was declared overnight. According to the CEC, Yanukovych had won the office of the presidency, by a margin of 49.5 percent to 46.6 percent.

How was the vote stolen? Where did Yanukovych's extra votes come from? According to Andrew Wilson in *Ukraine's Orange Revolution*, the fraud occurred primarily in east Ukraine. Nationwide, 80.7 percent of eligible voters, up 5 percent from the first round, voted in the runoff election. In east Ukraine, the official results had Yanukovych winning an astonishing 92 percent of the vote, compared with Yushchenko's 6 percent.

Where the Zoriany team truly excelled was in electronically falsifying the final vote count. In Yanukovych's home region of Donetsk, voter turnout was supposedly 96.7 percent, an impossibly high voter turnout. The vote count there was Yanukovych 96.2 percent to Yushchenko's 2 percent. In three constituencies in Donetsk, Yushchenko was officially recorded as having received only 0.6 percent of the vote.

In the eastern Ukraine industrial region known as the Donbas, which included the cities of Donetsk and Luhansk, Yanukovych supposedly received 1,000,000 more votes in the second round than he had in the first round. These extra votes alone were enough to secure his margin of victory.

It is out of the question that such a large increase in voter turnout actually occurred. The Zoriany group had done its job. The election that had been legitimately won by Viktor Yushchenko had been stolen, and Viktor Yanukovych would become the next president of Ukraine. Elections had been stolen before, with little or no protest from the Ukrainian people. This time, however, the people of Ukraine were determined to have their voices heard.

Viktor Yushchenko had called for a limited number of protestors to meet in Kiev's Independence Square, known as the "Maidan" after the polls closed at 8:00 P.M. on election night, Sunday, November 21. Yushchenko knew that election fraud was going to take place. He wanted a public forum to announce the results of the exit polls.

It was also assumed that the official vote count would take days (as it had in the first round), and Yushchenko wanted to have a parallel, public vote count as well. To everyone's surprise, between 25,000 and 30,000 people turned out with little organization or prior announcement. The Orange Revolution had begun.

The demonstration was dubbed "the Orange Revolution" because orange was the official color of Yushchenko's campaign. To show solidarity with Yushchenko's campaign, protestors wore orange ribbons and orange clothing and carried orange flags emblazoned with the slogan, "Yes! Yushchenko!"

Viktor Yushchenko speaks to a crowd in Independence Square in the Ukrainian capitol of Kiev, on November 22, 2004. During his speech, Yushchenko made accusations of electoral fraud.

On the morning of November 22, the official state-run Ukrainian media announced that Yanukovych was the winner of the election. At the same time, hundreds and thousands of leaflets were being printed, stating "Viktor Yushchenko Has Won! By 54 percent to 43 percent!" That day, an estimated 200,000–300,000 Kievites (citizens of Kiev) did not go to work. Instead, they crowded into the Maidan, spilling over into the adjoining main street.

The authorities were shocked at the public display of defiance. In addition, and just as important, the world media took notice. The media's attention made it much more difficult for authorities to use force to end the demonstrations. It also made it more difficult for authorities to continue to "cover up" their electoral fraud.

The number of protestors kept growing. A tent city sprang up in the Maidan, and donated food and supplies were given to the protestors. On November 23, an estimated half a million protestors peacefully marched in front of the Verkhovna Rada. Local authorities in Kiev and other cities refused to accept the legitimacy of the official election results. Finally, on that same day, in the half empty chamber of the rada, Yushchenko took the oath of office as president of Ukraine. He did this to symbolize that he was the actual winner and to show his determination to assume the role that he had rightfully won.

Protests continued to spread throughout the country. International response to the ongoing crisis grew stronger, as well. Colin Powell, who was then the United States secretary of state, strongly condemned the voter fraud. The government tried to ignore the protestors in the street and the condemnation of the world, however. On November 24, Viktor Yanukovych was officially certified as the winner of the election by the Central Election Committee.

The next morning, November 25, Yushchenko spoke publicly to his supporters in Kiev. He urged them to begin a series of mass protests across the nation. He asked them to begin a series of general strikes (wherein people refuse to go to work) and sit-ins. This was meant to keep the world's attention on Ukraine. It was also hoped that doing so would cripple the government and force it to concede defeat.

The protests, strikes, and sit-ins continued and grew, as more and more people took to the streets. It is estimated that more than one million protestors lined the streets of Kiev alone. The protests, filling the streets with enormous crowds

Viktor Yushchenko *(right)* walks with former Polish president Lech Walesa *(left)* at a rally in Kiev on November 25, 2004. Walesa traveled to Ukraine hoping to mediate the controversial presidential election involving Yushchenko and Yanukovych.

despite freezing winter temperatures, showed the government and the world the courage and determination of the Ukrainian people.

THE PROTESTS, FILLING THE STREETS WITH ENORMOUS CROWDS DESPITE FREEZING WINTER TEMPERATURES, SHOWED THE GOVERNMENT AND THE WORLD THE COURAGE AND DETERMINATION OF THE UKRAINIAN PEOPLE.

Throughout this period, Viktor Yushchenko and Yulia Tymoshenko played the roles of "good cop" and "bad cop." Yushchenko was the calm, statesman-like figure. He insisted that the protests stay peaceful and did his best to make sure there were no outbreaks of violence. Tymoshenko's role, on the other hand, was to stir the passions of the crowd. For example, she called for the protestors to take over the airports and train stations. She knew very well that this would not happen. By inciting the crowds, though, she managed to keep the government wary of possible armed insurrection.

The protests continued through December. On December 3, the Ukrainian Supreme Court broke the ongoing political deadlock. The Court decided that because of the massive scale of the electoral fraud, it was impossible to establish true election results. Therefore, it threw out the official government results that would have given the presidency to Yanukovych. Instead, the Court ordered a revote of the runoff, to be held on December 26, 2004. It was a victory for Yushchenko.

On December 8, the rada amended laws that cleared the way for the new elections to be held. Giving into both domestic and international pressure, they also passed new laws that made it far more difficult for government authorities to tamper with election results. As part of the package, however, because they knew that Yushchenko would win the new election, they also included laws that could weaken the power of the presidency.

Eager to resolve the situation, Yushchenko agreed to the new laws. Tymoshenko, though, argued that Yushchenko gave in to them too easily. She said that he shouldn't have compromised. She felt that because of the protestors they had on the streets, they still had leverage, and that Yushchenko gave away too much power too easily. Yushchenko felt that everything had to be done legally, by act of parliament, and, without parliamentary approval of new elections, the power struggle would have continued.

The third and final round of the 2004 presidential elections was held on December 26. To no one's surprise, Yushchenko won the election, with an official 52 percent of the vote, against Yanukovych's 44.2 percent. On hearing the final results, Yushchenko addressed the crowd, "This is a victory for the Ukrainian people, the Ukrainian nation. . . . This is what dozens of millions of Ukrainians dreamt about. Today, it is fashionable, stylish and beautiful to be a citizen of Ukraine."

After the election, the *New York Times* reported that Ukrainian security agencies played a part in helping the Orange Revolution succeed. These were the very same agencies that were controlled by President Kuchma and Prime Minister Yanukovych. It had been at a meeting with the SBU (the Security Service of Ukraine), where Yushchenko and his supporters asked the organization not to interfere with the elections on the side of the government, that Yushchenko was probably poisoned.

The *Times* reported that on November 28, more than 10,000 troops were to be sent in to stop the protests in Kiev. The commander of the military informed Yushchenko's team about what was soon to occur. Phone calls were made—from the SBU to Yushchenko aides, to the American ambassador to Colin Powell to President Kuchma. At the last minute, someone (it is unknown exactly who) gave the order to stop the attack against the protestors. Because of this, the Orange Revolution was allowed to continue to its peaceful and successful conclusion.

Before leaving office though, the Kuchma administration had some last-minute cleaning up to do. To gain time,

Yanukovych initiated a series of last-minute appeals with the courts about supposed irregularities and illegalities within the Yushchenko campaign. There was nothing to the complaints, but the appeals took time, pushing back the date of

On December 27, 2004, Viktor Yushchenko and Yulia Tymoshenko participate in a rally at Independence Square in Kiev. During this time, Yushchenko and Tymoshenko were close allies, working together for a fair electoral process.

Yushchenko's inauguration. This allowed the Kuchma administration more time to destroy possibly incriminating paperwork and to grab as much money as they could.

Properties owned by the state were sold at low prices to companies owned by members of the Kuchma administration. It is estimated that during November and December of 2004, $1.33 billion left the Ukraine. The government is alleged to have issued 200 passports with aliases for members of the outgoing administration. This would allow those who might be facing criminal prosecution under Yushchenko to easily flee the country without detection.

President Kuchma himself received a rather extravagant retirement package. He was to continue to receive his full presidential salary for life; free medical care; free use of government dacha #72, its staff, two cars, and four drivers; payment of half of his electric bills; and fees paid to retain one advisor and two assistants. All this was to be paid for by the state, by Ukrainian taxpayers, as long as he lived.

Viktor Yushchenko was inaugurated as Ukraine's first freely elected president on January 23, 2005, in Kiev. One month earlier, the *Ukrainian Weekly* reported that Yushchenko had addressed a crowd with these words, "During 14 years we were independent, but we were not free."

Through Viktor Yushchenko's unbelievable courage and determination, and with the backing and support of the Ukrainian people, a peaceful revolution had taken place. Viktor Yushchenko and his supporters now held the reins of governmental power. Would he be able to make the changes necessary to transform Ukraine into the true democracy he and his supporters wanted?

9

Aftermath

DURING THE FIRST 100 DAYS OF VIKTOR YUSHCHENKO'S PRESIDENCY, dramatic changes took place in Ukraine's government. As agreed to in the "Force of the People" declaration in July 2004, on January 24, Yushchenko nominated Yulia Tymoshenko as prime minister. On February 4, she was confirmed by the Verkhovna rada; she received a record-breaking 373 votes out of 450. Other Yushchenko allies were confirmed as well, so his people controlled the major levels of government.

Also on January 24, his first full day in office, President Yushchenko made his first official visit abroad. This trip was to Russia, to meet with President Vladimir Putin. Putin had been active in trying to get Yushchenko's rival, Viktor Yanukovych, elected as president. Russia was (and is) Ukraine's largest trading partner, however. Yushchenko knew that if he went personally to visit Putin, he would be better able to settle any differences between the two nations.

Viktor Yushchenko *(left)* traveled to Russia on January 24, 2005, one day after taking office, to meet with Russian president, Vladimir Putin *(right)*. The goal was to smooth out relations between the two countries. Putin had been a big supporter of Yushchenko's rival, Viktor Yanukovych.

Russia was just the first of many trips overseas for Yushchenko. He visited the European Parliament in Strasbourg in February, and he traveled to the United States in April. Indeed, by mid-April, he had spent his office's entire annual travel budget! The travel served a definite purpose, though. By visiting Western nations and their leaders, he illustrated his commitment to achieving closer ties between his country and the West.

Next, Yushchenko made immediate moves to root out corruption in the Ukrainian government. He declared that his new government "will not steal," and that business and politics would remain separate. He cut taxes and moved to eliminate tax privileges for wealthy businessowners and their businesses.

At the end of April, Yushchenko's popularity remained high, and 47.4 percent of the population believed that the country was moving in the right direction. Compare this to the numbers from September 2004, when only 26 percent thought that Ukraine was moving in the right direction, and 54 percent thought it was definitely moving the wrong way.

Yushchenko also made efforts to form new international alliances. Since he took office, Ukraine has applied for membership in the World Trade Organization (WTO), the European Union (EU), and the North American Treaty Organization (NATO). Membership in these organizations would serve to strengthen Ukraine's economy, as well as its political and military ties to the West.

In addition, in August 2005, Yushchenko joined with Georgian president Mikhail Saakashvili and signed the Borjomi Declaration. This agreement called for the creation of a new organization for international cooperation, the Community of Democratic Choice (CDC). It would bring together the democracies and developing democracies around the Baltic, Black, and Caspian seas—all former Soviet states. The CDC met for the first time in Kiev, on December 1–2, 2005.

Things seemed to be going well for the Yushchenko administration, but progress soon faltered. Once revolutionaries, even in a peaceful revolution like the Orange Revolution, achieve power, it can be difficult to hold them together. As members of what was once the opposition, they are united in their desire for change, but they often begin to quarrel among themselves once they are in power. This is what happened in Ukraine.

On September 8, 2005, President Viktor Yushchenko dismissed his entire government, including Prime Minister Yulia Tymoshenko. He explained his reasons in an interview with Larry King, posted on his Web site, http://www.president.gov.ua/en/news/data/17_3003.html:

Well, they were partners, actually, in the revolution—we stood together in Independence Square. But despite this, we all represented different political forces. I brought her to power. I gave her a lot of authority. I gave a lot of authority to the Prime Minister, to the State Secretary, to the Secretary to the National Security and Defense Council. Then later on some kind of misunderstanding appeared among the members of the team and finally we got like zero level of trust between the members of the team. There were different reasons for that.

Some of them believed that another side was taking too much authority. Some of them regarded that the other side was working actually for public than for the benefit of the country. Some decided to use personal interest, and those personal interests prevailed over state interest. And that was in full contradiction with the ideas that were declared in the Independence Square, and that was not my policy. That was not my type of aspiration.

And when I noticed that this kind of conflict emerged, I dedicated a lot of time in order to make them stretch their hands to each other. Well, to make it shortly, it didn't happen. And that is why I didn't—I didn't want the crisis of interpersonal relations to be transferred into political crisis or even worse crisis.

And that is why with all my respect to them, I told them that the other people should come to the authority, should come to the power. You will remain my partners, you will remain my friends, but what you are doing does not correspond to my concept of the development of the country and to my obligations as the obligations of president.

There was more involved than just the inability of the cabinet members to get along with one another. Yushchenko believed that Prime Minister Tymoshenko had made mistakes concerning matters of economic policy. The way that companies were reprivatized brought about distrust from the business community. A gasoline crisis caused prices to skyrocket. There seemed to be a new crisis each month. Changes would have to be made.

Tymoshenko was not happy with her dismissal. She claimed that she was dismissed not because of her policies but because she was too popular and posed a threat to Yushchenko. After her dismissal, she resurrected her own political bloc and began to tour the country in preparation for the 2006 parliamentary elections. She made it very clear that she planned to return to the position of prime minister.

Yushchenko named Yury I. Yekhanurov as acting prime minister on September 8, 2005. Yulia Tymoshenko (who still held her seat in parliament) and her voting bloc opposed his candidacy. On the first round of voting on September 20, Yekhanurov was 3 votes short of the 226 votes needed for approval. In desperation, President Yushchenko turned to his one-time political foe, Viktor Yanukovych.

In exchange for his support and the votes of his regions of Ukraine voting bloc, President Yushchenko was forced to give in to several demands: Criminal investigations by the government of Yanukovych's supporters would come to an end. President Yushchenko also agreed to diminish the power of the new National Security and Defense Council. The NSDC was a new agency active in investigating governmental corruption. With those concessions to Yanukovych made, Yushchenko got the votes he needed to get his new government approved.

Yushchenko paid a political price for this deal. Many of his allies thought that he had betrayed the Orange Revolution by allying himself with Viktor Yanukovych. Yushchenko is a practical politician; he knew that he had to get a new government in place if he wanted to accomplish his goals, and if he had to make a deal with Yanukovych to get it done, then so be it.

Yushchenko faced other political problems at the end of 2005. Ukraine is dependent on Russia for its supply of oil and natural gas; in December 2005, Russian president Vladimir Putin threatened to cut off supplies of natural gas to Ukraine. He said he would do so unless Ukraine agreed to pay a price increase of nearly 300 percent over what their contracts said they should pay.

Yushchenko was outraged by the Russian demands. Negotiations soon fell apart. On Sunday, January 1, 2006, Putin made good on his threats, and Russia cut off Ukraine's supply of natural gas. The world was outraged (about 80 percent of Europe's natural gas is shipped through Ukraine). Three days later, on January 4, Russia and Ukraine reached a compromise, and shipments of natural gas resumed.

According to the terms of the agreement, Ukraine's gas bill would nearly double by 2007. An offshore company, called RusUkrEnergo will be the exclusive supplier of Ukraine's natural gas. The company, half owned by Gazprom (Russia's natural gas company) and half owned by an Austrian-based company with unknown beneficiaries, will buy gas from Russia for $230 per 1,000 cubic meters. Ukraine will then buy the gas from that company for $95 per 1,000 cubic meters. Supposedly, the price difference will be made up because the company will sell Ukraine more Central Asian natural gas, which is less expensive than Russian gas.

Many critics spoke out against the deal. They pointed out that RusUkrEnergo had been investigated for ties to organized crime. According to the *New York Times*, the head of Ukraine's national security service, Oleksandr Turchynov, said that he urged Yushchenko to prosecute the company but, instead, was removed from his job.

The agreement and resulting political firestorm only added to Yushchenko's political problems. Many observers felt that

Conflicts over gas prices between Ukraine and state-owned, Russian gas supplier Gazprom began in 2005. In January 2006, Gazprom cut its gas exports to Ukraine when the two parties could not come to an agreement. Here, Viktor Yushchenko *(center)* leads a meeting concerning the counry's gas issues on January 1, 2006.

the mysteries relating to RusUkrEnergo—Who actually owns it? How was the company chosen?—reflect the kind of corrupt business dealings that the Orange Revolution was supposed to bring to an end.

Others pointed out that one of Putin's reasons for starting the whole energy crisis was to make Yushchenko's government look bad. Parliamentary elections would be coming up in March, and Putin was eager to do anything he could to help his ally, Viktor Yanukovych, gain a majority in the new parliament.

The parliament was also unhappy about the deal. On January 10, 2005, the Verkhovna rada passed a vote of "no confidence" in the government. President Yushchenko dismissed the vote as a "publicity stunt by the opposition."

Two months later, on March 6, parliamentary elections were held. In a stunning reversal of fortune, Viktor Yanukovych's Party of Regions came in first place, with 32.14 percent of the vote. Bloc Yulia Tymoshenko came in second with 22.29 percent of the vote. President Viktor Yushchenko's bloc, Our Ukraine, came in third place, with only 13.95 percent of the vote.

It was a remarkable defeat for Viktor Yushchenko because it came only a little over a year after coming to power in the Orange Revolution. Negotiations began to form a new government. Yushchenko, dealing from a position of political weakness, wanted to find a candidate who would be acceptable enough to reunite all the warring factions of the old Orange Revolution allies.

Negotiations continued for more than four months. Alliances were made and unmade. At one point, a tentative agreement was reached between Yushchenko's party and that of former prime minister Yulia Tymoshenko. This agreement would have returned Tymoshenko to the office of prime minister.

Unfortunately, the arrangement fell apart. Lawmakers opposed to the coalition physically barricaded the podium to block a vote that would have finalized the new government. Ultimately, the Socialist Party leader, Oleksandr O. Moroz, left the coalition and joined with Viktor Yanukovich's Party of Regions.

With this move, Viktor Yushchenko was left with no alternative. On August 3, 2006, he nominated his former rival, Viktor Yanukovich, to become the new prime minister of Ukraine. Under the terms of the "nonbinding" agreement between the two men, President Yushchenko retains power over foreign and

On August 3, 2006, Viktor Yushchenko nominated his former rival, Viktor Yanukovich, to become the new prime minister of Ukraine.

defense policy. Viktor Yanukovich, in turn, pledged to pursue Yushchenko's main policy goals, including cooperation with NATO and the West. How long this coalition can remain intact is anybody's guess.

There were many factors that went into Our Ukraine's poor showing in the 2006 parliamentary elections. Yushchenko's firing of his initial government headed by Yulia Tymoshenko was one factor. The problem he had installing his new government and the questions over the natural gas deal all played their parts, as well.

There was also a lack of patience at the perceived slowness of Yushchenko's government to clean up and remedy the corruption of the previous regime. After a revolution, change never comes as quickly as its supporters hope. In addition, problems brought on by Yushchenko himself probably added to the impatience of the Ukrainian voters.

The lack of justice in the case of Georgiy Gongadze was one such situation. Georgiy Gongadze was the publisher of the online journal *Ukrainska Pravda*. He was a brave and courageous journalist and considered to be a champion of the Ukrainian people against the corruption and brutality of the Kuchma regime.

On September 5, 2000, Gongadze filed a report about one of President Kuchma's confidantes. On the night of September 16, he disappeared. Fifty days later, his dead body was found in a shallow grave. He had been beheaded, probably with an axe. While Kuchma was president, no charges were ever filed, witnesses were murdered, and suspects were allowed to leave the country.

One of Viktor Yushchenko's campaign promises was to bring the killers of Georgiy Gongadze to justice. He promised Ukrainians that the case would reach the courts by May 2005. The trial of the accused killers (but not the persons who gave the orders for Gongadze to be killed) began in February 2006.

Many Ukrainians felt that Yushchenko was not doing all he could to get the case resolved. It is considered fact by many Ukrainians that President Kuchma himself ordered the kidnapping and murder and has been using the long delays to pay off people whose knowledge may help solve the crime. As of May 2006, the case is being appealed. Many people fear that the people truly responsible for the killing will never be brought to justice.

Political problems caused by members of Yushchenko's own family were another factor in Our Ukraine's losses. In July 2005, the name of Yushchenko's 19-year-old son, Andriy, was splashed across headlines all across Ukraine. According to Mosnews.com, Andriy Yushchenko drives a brand new BMW, valued at $120,000. He owns a Vertu cell phone with a platinum body worth about $30,000. He also, according to Mosnews, pays the headwaiters at expensive Ukraine restaurants large amounts of cash to get himself the best table in the house. According to Nikolai Katerinchuk, Ukraine's deputy head of the country's tax inspectorate, Andriy's annual income is almost $100 million. Where does the money come from?

Apparently, the money comes from the sale of Orange Revolution memorabilia. After winning the election, President Yushchenko gave his son all property rights for Orange Revolution memorabilia. The continuing popularity of T-shirts, flags, and other items with the symbol of the Orange Revolution has made him a very rich young man. For every sale of anything "Orange Revolution," Andriy makes money.

To many Ukrainians, Andriy's enormous wealth symbolizes another broken promise of the Orange Revolution. Once

The Ukrainian press has written extensively about Andriy Yushchenko's extravagant lifestyle. He reportedly drives fast expensive cars; lives in a lavish apartment; and has bodyguards trailing his every move.

again, someone politically well-connected got rich at the expense of others. In addition, it didn't seem right for the son of the president to be flaunting his wealth in a country where so many are still very poor. Yushchenko has had a hard time defending his son's actions. His love for his son makes him want to protect him. To many Ukrainians, it appears that he condones his son's activities.

Although things haven't always gone as well as he had hoped, there have been bright spots during Yushchenko's presidency. On April 5, 2005, Yushchenko was presented the Profile in Courage Award given by the John F. Kennedy Library Foundation. The award is considered one of the most prestigious awards that can be given to a politician. It was named for U.S. president John F. Kennedy's Pulitzer Prize–winning book, *Profiles in Courage.* It is presented to political figures who show positive courage "and stand up for the public interest, even when it is not in their interest to do so." The award has been given mainly to Americans. It is a rare honor for it to be presented to a foreign official.

Yushchenko was greatly honored to be given an award named for one of his political heroes, John F. Kennedy. Few people alive today are as worthy of the honor as Viktor Yushchenko. As the award committee said in their announcement of his award, "In December of 2004, despite an assassination attempt and repeated efforts by Russian-backed political opponents to rig his defeat by electoral fraud, Viktor Yushchenko became the democratically elected leader of Ukraine. In doing so, he inspired citizens of the world with his extraordinary courage."

President Viktor Yushchenko continues to inspire the world with his courage. Despite the attempted assassination, election fraud, and political and personal problems, he continues to believe in the ideals of the Orange Revolution. As he said in his acceptance speech for his Profile in Courage Award, "We were led by the . . . desire to free Ukrainians from poverty and lawlessness, reaffirm justice and the rule of law. We want to make Ukraine one of the leaders of democracy, a flourishing nation among European peoples."

August 4, 2006, Ukrainian president Viktor Yushchenko shakes hands with Viktor Yanukovych after Parliament appointed the former presidential candidate prime minister of Ukraine. The two former rivals now must work together to lead the country.

The task facing Viktor Yushchenko and the Ukrainian people is enormous. To transform Ukraine from the country it was to the nation Viktor Yushchenko dreams it can be will be the work of several generations. It will take time, patience, and determination. Thanks to the courage of Yushchenko, though, Ukraine is now on the right path. Free and honest elections are held, and the people are on their way toward a truly free and democratic future. As Yushchenko said in an interview with the German newspaper *Der Spiegel,* "Through the events we call the Orange Revolution, Ukraine became a different country. Today, nobody has hopes of coming to power on the basis of election fraud and nobody can oppress journalists any longer. There is no return to yesterday." For that, the people of Ukraine will always owe their thanks to the courage of Viktor Yushchenko.

CHRONOLOGY

988 A.D.   Grand Duke Volodymyr converts himself and his Kievan Rus' Empire from paganism to Orthodox Christianity.

1240   Kiev falls to Mongol armies.

1569   Following Union of Lubin, much of the western area of Ukrainian Territory is given over to Polish control.

1654   Treaty of Pereyaslav is signed: Cossacks accept Russian protection, thus opening the door to nearly 350 years of Russian domination of Ukraine.

1686   Kiev and all lands east of the Dnieper River fall under Russian control. Western Ukraine gradually moves from Polish control to Austrian.

1876   Edict of Ens bans the use of the Ukrainian language throughout Ukrainian territory controlled by Russia.

1922   In the aftermath of World War I, western Ukraine (Galicia) is given over to the Second Polish Republic. The majority of the country, now called the Ukrainian Soviet Socialist Republic becomes part of the USSR— the Union of Soviet Socialist Republics.

1932–1933   The Great Famine: Soviet Premier Joseph Stalin orders the collectivization of Ukrainian farms and dramatically increases production quotas. Because of his deliberate policies, millions of Ukrainians starve to death.

1941   Nazi Germany invades Ukraine. The Jewish population is massacred as part of Hitler's "Final Solution," and many Ukrainians are sent to Germany to work as slave labor. Between 5 and 6 million Ukrainian civilians are killed during World War II.

1954 Viktor Andriiovych Yushchenko is born in Khoruzhivka, Sumy Oblast, Ukraine, on February 23.

1975 Viktor Yushchenko graduates from Ternopil Finance and Economics Institute with degree in accounting.

1975–1976 Yushchenko serves in Soviet army, positioned on the Soviet-Turkish Border.

1976–1986 Yushchenko begins his career in banking.

1987 Yushchenko moves to Kiev and comes under patronage of Vadym Hetman. His career in banking begins to flourish.

1991 Ukraine declares independence from the Soviet Union.

1993 Viktor Yushchenko becomes head of the National Bank of Ukraine (NBU); makes great strides in improving Ukraine's economy.

1998 Marries Kateryna Chumachenko. They eventually have three children: daughters Sophia and Chrystyna, and son Taras.

1999 Viktor Yushchenko becomes prime minister of Ukraine.

2001 After a no-confidence vote by parliament, Yushchenko is forced to step down as prime minister.

2002 In parliamentary elections, Viktor Yushchenko's political coalition, "Our Ukraine," wins more votes than any other bloc; signals the birth of a new opposition to the government of President Leonid Kuchma.

2004	*July 4.* Viktor Yushchenko formally announces his candidacy for the presidency of Ukraine on July 4.
2004	*September 6.* After a late dinner with the head of Security Service of Ukraine (SBU), Yushchenko becomes seriously ill; tests later find he had been poisoned by high levels of dioxins.
2004	*October 31.* Despite electoral fraud, Viktor Yushchenko leads first round of presidential elections, with 39.9 percent of the vote. He enters run-off election with Viktor Yanukovych, the government's candidate, who won 39.3 percent of vote.
2004	*November 21.* Yushchenko leads by a comfortable margin in reliable exit polls, but because of alleged massive election fraud, Viktor Yanukovych wins the official vote count, by 49.5 percent to 46.6 percent.
2004	*November 22.* Supporters of Viktor Yushchenko, protesting the stolen election, begin to fill the streets of Kiev. The protests spread throughout Ukraine. The Orange Revolution has begun.
2004	*December 3.* The Ukraine Supreme Court throws out the results of the November 21 runoff election, citing massive voter fraud. The court orders a new runoff election to be held.
2004	*December 26.* Viktor Yushchenko is elected as president of Ukraine.
2005	*September 8.* Because of what he saw as disarray, President Yushchenko dismisses his entire government, including Prime Minister Yulia Tymoshenko.

2005–2006	*December–January.* Russian president Vladimir Putin announces a 300 percent increase in the price of natural gas sold by Russia to Ukraine. Negotiations fail, and Russia cuts off natural gas supplies on January 1, 2005. On January 4, a new agreement is reached, and the sale of natural gas resumes.
March 6, 2006	"Our Ukraine" political bloc comes in a distant third in parliamentary elections, behind both Viktor Yankovych's and Yulia Tymoshenko's parties. Attempts to form a new government begin.

BIBLIOGRAPHY

"Biography, Hobbies and Interviews," My Ukraine: Personal Web site of Viktor Yushchenko. Available online. URL: www .yushchenko.com.ua/eng.

"Biography: Kateryna Yushchenko," Official Web site of President of Ukraine. Available online. URL: www.president.gov .ua/en/content/p_600_e.html.

Bohush, Ilona. "An Interview with Kateryna Yushchenko: I Have Always Feared for Viktor, But I Never Even Imagined That His Enemies Would Carry It This Far." My Ukraine: Personal Web site of Viktor Yushchenko: Family. Available online. URL: http://www.yuschenko.com.ua/eng/Private/ Family/1224/. October 2, 2004.

"History of Ukraine," Wikipedia. Available online. URL: http://en.wikipedia.org/wiki/History_of_Ukraine. Updated on September 5, 2006.

"Holodomor," Wikipedia. http://en.wikipedia.org/wiki/ Holodomor. Updated on September 4, 2006.

Kharchenko, Tetyana. "Viktor Yushchenko's 50th Birthday Interview," *The Action Ukraine Report*. Available online. URL: http://artukraine.com/buildukraine/yushchenko23 .htm. February 21, 2004.

King, Larry. "An Interview with Viktor Yushchenko," September 18, 2005. Official Web site of President of Ukraine. Available online. URL: www.president.gov.ua/en/news/data/ print/3003.html.

Kramer, Andrew E., and C.J. Chivers. "Russia and Ukraine Reach Compromise on Natural Gas." *The New York Times* (January 5, 2006).

Mayr, Walter, and Christian Neef. "Interview with Ukrainian President Viktor Yushchenko: 'There Is No Return to Yesterday,'" Spiegel Online International. Available online. URL: www.spiegel.de/international/0,1518,392426,00.html. Updated on December 27, 2005.

Myers, Steven Lee. "6 Weeks After Ukrainian Vote, It's Unclear Who Won," *The New York Times* (May 13, 2006).

———. "Ukraine Parliament Approves New Premier After Rival's Deal," *The New York Times*, (September 23, 2005).

Myers, Steven Lee, and Andrew E. Kramer. "Gas Deal Roils Ukraine and May Have Cut Leader's Vote," *The New York Times* (March 30, 2006).

"Orange Revolution," Wikipedia. Available online. URL: http://en.wikipedia.org/wiki/Orange_Revolution. Updated August on 29, 2006.

Piasecki, Waldemar. "Interview with Ukrainian Presidential Candidate Viktor Yushchenko," Ukrainian Community Press Releases. Available online. URL: www.brama.com/news/press/2004/11/041108wp_yushchenko-interview.html. Updated on November 8, 2004.

"President of Ukraine," Wikipedia. Available online. URL: http://en.wikipedia.org/wiki/President_of_Ukraine. Updated on September 3, 2006.

Reid, Anna. *Borderland: A Journey Through the History of Ukraine.* Boulder, Colo.: Westview Press, 2000.

"Ukraine," Wikipedia. Available online. URL: http://en.wikipedia.org/wiki/Ukraine. Updated on September 5, 2006.

"Ukrainian Presidential Election, 2004," Wikipedia. Available online. URL: http://en.wikipedia.org/wiki/Ukrainian_ presidential_elections%2C_2004. Updated on August 12, 2006.

"Ukrainization," Wikipedia. Available online. URL: http://en.wikipedia.org/wiki/Ukrainization. Updated on August 30, 2006.

"Viktor Yanukovych," Wikipedia. Available online. URL: http://wikipedia.org/wiki/Viktor_Yanukovich. Updated on August 17, 2006.

"Viktor Yushchenko," Wikipedia. Available online. URL: http://en.wikipedia.org/wiki/Viktor_Yushchenko. Updated on September 2, 2006.

"Viktor Yushchenko," Notablebiographies.com. Available online. URL: www.notablebiographies.com/news/Sh-Z/ Yushchenko-Viktor.html.

Wilson, Andrew. *Ukraine's Orange Revolution.* New Haven, Conn.: Yale University Press, 2005.

"Yulia Tymoshenko," Wikipedia. Available online. URL: http:// en.wikipedia.org/wiki/Yulia_Tymoshenko.

Zorya, Vasyl. "Interview: Kateryna Chumachenko Yushchenko on Life in Ukraine, and as a Politician's Wife," *The Ukrainian Weekly.* Available online. URL: www.ukrweekly.com/ Archive/2002/100208.shtml.

FURTHER READING

BOOKS

Cheney, Glenn Alan. *Chernobyl: The Ongoing Story of the World's Deadliest Nuclear Disaster.* New York: Macmillan, 1993.

Malamud, Bernard. *The Fixer.* New York: Farrar, Straus and Giroux, 2004.

Oparenko, Christina. *Ukrainian Folk-tales.* Oxford, UK: Oxford University Press, 1996.

Otfinoski, Steven. *Ukraine (Nations in Transition)* 2nd ed. New York: Facts on File, 2004.

Reed, Anna. *Borderland: A Journey Through the History of Ukraine.* Boulder, Colo.: Westview Press, 2000.

Suhl, Yuri. *Uncle Misha's Partisans.* New York: Shapolsky, 1985.

Tal, Eve. *Double Crossing.* El Paso, Tex.: Cinco Puntos Press, 2005.

Walker, Linda. *Living After Chernobyl: Ira's Story.* Milwaukee, Wisc.: World Almanac Library (Gareth Stevens), 2005.

WEB SITES
President of Ukraine official Web site:
http://www.president.gov.ua/en.
Personal Web site of Viktor Yushchenko:
http://www.yushchenko.com.ua/eng.

Photo Credits

INDEX

About the Authors

DENNIS ABRAMS attended Antioch College, where he majored in English and communications. Abrams is a freelance writer who has written many biographies for young adult readers. He lives in Houston, Texas.

ARTHUR M. SCHLESINGER, JR. is the leading American historian of our time. He won the Pulitzer Prize for his books *The Age of Jackson* (1945) and *A Thousand Days* (1965), which also won the National Book Award. Professor Schlesinger is the Albert Schweitzer Professor of the Humanities at the City University of New York and has been involved in several other Chelsea House projects, including the series *Revolutionary War Leaders*, *Colonial Leaders*, and *Your Government*.